Colin Spencer's

SUMMER COOKING

D1315264

By the same author
CORDON VERT
MEDITERRANEAN VEGETARIAN COOKING
THE ROMANTIC VEGETARIAN

Edited by the author
GREEN CUISINE

Colin Spencer's
SUMMER COOKING

Edited by Lee Faber

Illustrated by Paul Davies

Thorsons
An Imprint of HarperCollins*Publishers*

Thorsons
An Imprint of HarperCollins*Publishers*
77-85 Fulham Palace Road,
Hammersmith, London W6 8JB

Published by Thorsons as *Al Fresco* 1987
Paperback edition, revised and expanded, 1992
1   3   5   7   9   10   8   6   4   2

© Colin Spencer 1987, 1992

Colin Spencer asserts the moral right to
be identified as the author of this work

A catalogue record for this book
is available from the British Library

ISBN 0 7225 2653 9

Typeset by Harper Phototypesetters Limited,
Northampton, England
Printed in Great Britain by Bath Press Ltd, Bath, Avon

All rights reserved. No part of this publication may be
reproduced, stored in a retrieval system, or transmitted,
in any form or by any means, electronic, mechanical,
photocopying, recording or otherwise, without the prior
permission of the publishers.

CONTENTS

All styling and Photography by Sue Atkinson, Mike Roles Studios.
Home Economists Elaine Andrews and Lucy Knox.

Thanks for loan of tableware/china to:
    The Token House, Windsor
    The Reject China Shop, Knightsbridge, London
    The Pine Place, St Leonard's Road, Windsor.

Thanks for loan of binoculars and shooting stick to:
    Windsor Guns & Field Sports.

Thanks for loan of hats and gloves to:
    Occasions, Peascod Street, Windsor
    The Gaslight Gaieties, Maidenhead.

Thanks for loan of marble to:
    The Fireplace Centre, All Saints Road, Maidenhead.

Locations for photography including:
    Oakley Court Hotel, Oakley Green, Bray.

INTRODUCTION

THE FOODS OF SUMMER

Summer seduces the palate and pleases the eye with such a variety of fresh fruits and vegetables, that it is no chore at all to eat vegetarian. Besides, these long hot days require modest sustenance, we eat lightly and summer vegetables fit our nutritional requirements exactly. Fresh garden vegetables include broad and green beans, peas and mange tout, the first tiny courgettes with their flowers, the first English green peppers, a range of lettuces, also endive, chicory, radicchio, while the herb garden is just beginning to flower; there is basil (the cook's favourite herb, the leaves to be torn in pieces, not chopped) and chervil, chives, coriander and lovage are all marvellous for adding to vegetable salads or for flavouring purées. There are also, of course, the great British standbys, mint and parsley, and now Hamburg parsley, the loose-leafed kind is just as available as the curly crisp type.

July is the most fruitful month, not only English strawberries, but raspberries, and loganberries, the latter continuing throughout August and into the blackberry season. Then there are also all those wonderful tiny currant fruits, red, black and white, some of these can be scattered in salads made from cereals and herbs so that the dish resembles a richly worked tapestry. Amongst this cornucopia I could not forget gooseberries, and how good purées made from these sharp-flavoured fruits are a fine foil with grilled fish; for I also have to mention, slipping from my vegetarian crusade, that July is quite the best month for crab, lobster, prawns and shrimps. It is also the month for grilse – young salmon – sometimes passed off to the customer by unscruplous or ignorant fishmongers as sea trout.

But I have forgotten another major fruit – cherries – eaten, often, from the bag, before you reach home. But if you can bother to stone them, they too can be added to salads or made into a refreshingly sharp cold soup. Fruit soups have never quite taken off, but in the summer heat they make a wonderful start to lunch or dinner, and they look ravishing and taste of ambrosia. Hungarian recipes often mix the fruit with yoghurt or sour cream which makes the dish too heavy. A starter should invigorate the appetite, never appease it.

Such gourmet summer pleasures are not only an *embarras de richesses* but *du choix* as well, but do not be bewildered and open a packet instead. It would be a crime at this time of year. First, make certain every ingredient is fresh and at its peak, pick over the fruit and vegetables before choosing what to buy, do not be frightened to make a fuss. You, the consumer are important, do not be browbeaten by barrow-boy or supermarket. The habit of wrapping portions of vegetables and fruits in clingwrap produces their own mini-greenhouse climate which if there are flaws in the produce will hasten its decline. So inspect all wrapped produce with care. So much of what is in season can be enjoyed raw, or with the smallest amount of blanching or cooking. I have never forgotten my first trip to Greece and eating raw broad beans from the pod at a quayside taverna at Rhodes. Peas from the pod are excellent too, as are mange tout eaten raw and whole. (However, these imported mange tout that you can buy early in the year have been grown from heavy doses of nitrate fertiliser and are forced in greenhouses; sadly they are totally without flavour. Do not confuse good summer English produce grown organically with this inferior product.) Crudités is as good a course as any to start a meal, especially an al fresco lunch, with the selected cut vegetables sprinkled only with a little sea salt and lemon juice, alternating pieces of carrot, pepper or courgette with crisp and variegated leaves, arranged as a huge platter in the centre of a table. Friends, guests and family can linger over this for as long as it takes to prepare the next course. You can, of course, add a flavoured mayonnaise in which people scoop or dip the crudites. Alternatively, tapenade made from black olives or melitzane made from baked aubergines would not have the cholesterol level of the mayonnaise, and the tapenade in particular has a marvellous swarthy voluptuousness upon the palate which changes every carrot stick into instant *dolce vita*.

July also just happens to be one of the best months for goat's milk cheese from either Britain or France, so another good starter – or a simple lunch or supper – is a slice of grilled chèvre, cooked so that it just begins to run, laid on a bed of fresh salad leaves, herbs and, almost *de rigeur*, rocket. For chèvre and rocket leaves are an indispensable pair. Goats, of course, are fond of rocket, but then they are so completely omnivorous they consume almost all in their path. (I kept a goat for a year, he occasionally got free and ate the clematis, roses and honeysuckle, but the day he demolished the parsley bed was the last straw and I sold him.

If you decide to turn this summer cornucopia into hot or warm dishes, keep the cooking simple; fresh boiled vegetables can be tossed in a little fromage frais and be the filling for pancakes, or turned into a sauce for a pasta dish, green beans can be sprinkled with roasted pine nuts or a mixture of fried breadcrumbs and garlic. Young globe artichokes are best halved or quartered and fried in olive oil and garlic, or simply halved and simmered with broad beans and a little white wine, then thickened with a little *beurre manié* (flour and good butter mixed into a paste and added to the stock in olive size pieces until you have reached the thickness required) with, at the last moment, chopped parsley added. Oh what bliss such a dish is.

A diet of salad vegetables and fruits may be excellent for the figure but might tend to leave a yawning gap in the appetite, and nutritionally such a diet should be balanced with some intake of cereal. Good bread will do, of course, and if you bake your own, tasty additions like herbs, cheese, olives and walnuts to the dough itself make wonderful summer loaves, especially if eaten warm, soon after they are baked. But I also like to make salads out of cereals, based on the Middle Eastern tabbouleh. This is made from cracked wheat, also termed bulgar wheat; and often confused, I fear, with buckwheat (which is not a wheat at all, or even a cereal, as it is related to rhubarb and sorrel.) Perhaps the easiest way to remember is that bulgar wheat is used extensively in the Middle East, its most famous dish being tabbouleh, while buckwheat is a staple of Russia, used as buckwheat flour in blinis and as an accompaniment (kasha to beef stroganoff rather than rice). As far as their suitability for summer salads goes, bulgar wheat needs no cooking, merely soaking, while buckwheat needs ten minutes simmering. I have also used millet as a summer salad, and though a reviewer of one of my cookery books considered I was offering nothing less than budgie fodder, millet makes a tasty dish, hot or cold and needs very little cooking – just quiet simmering for twenty minutes. Couscous is yet another grain which needs little preparation and twenty minutes steaming. All these cereal salads need after cooking or soaking is to be tossed in a good garlicky vinaigrette with added lemon juice and plenty of chopped herbs, parsley, mint or chives.

If you are fortunate enough to have an excess of broad beans or garden peas and have grown bored with eating them raw or cooked, make either beautiful purées or moulds. The garden peas, reduced to a purée, turn into the most vibrant green and are a sybaritic delight used as a stuffing in cannelloni or lasagne, or with an added egg baked in small ramekins, then left to cool before unmoulding. Broad beans will happily adjust to the same treatment; in fact there is a famous Sardinian dish – faiscedda – where the beans are reduced to a purée, mixed with eggs, a few breadcrumbs, a pinch of nutmeg and cinnamon, formed into a large flat cake and fried in olive oil.

As for those shellfish which are nearly always bought ready boiled from the fishmonger, I have reached the conclusion after being tempted in the last thirty years to many a cooked dish flamed in brandy with wine and cheese sauces, that shellfish are all best cold. The reason why you buy shellfish ready-cooked is that unless they are cooked immediately after catching the brains become very quickly toxic; this is why when you do buy uncooked prawns (generally a pale jade in colour) they are both headless and frozen. (If raw and with their heads on they must have been irradiated and labelled as such.) If you do chance to find them, there is one Portuguese recipe which is a triumph of simplicity. It can be made with the large ready-boiled Mediterranean prawns, but it is best with the uncooked ones. Peel the shell from the prawns and pour some olive oil into a terracotta baking dish, break up one red chilli and scatter it into the oil, then peel and slice about six to ten garlic cloves, turn the prawns in the oil, so they are covered and insert the sliced garlic wherever you can. Bake in a very hot oven for ten to fifteen minutes. Soak up the olive oil with good crusty bread.

Eaten cold, lobster, prawns and crab, of course, need a little sauce and quite often it is a flavoured mayonnaise; chilli would be my choice with a hint of garlic. Slightly less fattening alternatives are sauces made from fromage frais or smetana and a good summer sauce with lobster is simply yoghurt with masses of finely chopped mint, chives, parsley and basil to cut across the richness of the flesh. The small brown shrimp, caught off our coasts at this time of year can be eaten whole, legs, head and tail and the more remarkable the flavour is, for they seem the very essence of the sea itself. If you cannot manage to pop them whole into your mouth, much as other people eat roasted cicadas or raw witchetty grub, it is permissable to snap off the head and tail.

WILD FOODS OF SUMMER

It is possible to pick your own salad when you are in the country or on the coast, or at least to augment it by brightening up the lettuce leaves with a variety of wild foods. It is best to study the pages of a good book on the subject (such as Richard Mabey's *Food for Free* or Joy Larkcom's *The Salad Garden*) and to learn first to recognize the leaves in your own garden. Many of the most tiresome weeds are edible. For many years, I have been fighting a losing battle with ground elder, which is taking over my country garden; but it is amazingly tasty to eat, having a slight aniseed flavour, and a few leaves, mixed with lettuce, make a pleasant salad. (I only wich I could eat it all.) Some other salad plants I list below.

Dandelion leaves are excellent. They are best picked and eaten when young; old dandelion is a bit tough.

Prickly Sowthistle is a little like dandelion and is very common.

Shepherd's Purse, another common weed, is another excellent salad leaf, rich in Vitamin C. It is cultivated in China.

Claytonia, Wild Sorrel, Lady's Mantle, Common Comfrey, Chickweed, Common Orache, Sea Purslane and Fat Hen can all be found in the common hedgerow. There are many others; Joy Larkcom lists thirty varieties in her book.

Shellfish

Although you can find winkles and cockles on the beaches, both require at least 12 hours of soaking in fresh water before they are boiled to get rid of the sand, so they are not suitable for an impromptu picnic.

But mussels are. They can be picked from rocks and breakwaters, the open ones discarded, the barnacles scraped off with a sharp knife, then boiled in a little water and white wine for a few minutes until they open.

Any mussels that remain closed after boiling must be thrown away.

The best mussels I have ever tasted were a small variety that looked more like clams. We ate them in Senegal on the banks of the River Gambia where the tree roots were clustered with these molluscs – we hacked a root away and took it back to camp, where we put the whole root over a fire, steamed the mussels and ate them hot.

You can occasionally find both clams and scallops on British beaches at low tide. The shells have to be prised open with a strong knife, then the clam or scallop is cut away and the rest discarded. The flesh should be washed briefly in cold water, then fried or steamed.

A word of warning about where to pick shellfish: do not gather them near a sewage outlet or anywhere there are signs of pollution. Make sure the shellfish are all alive before being prepared or cooked (if the shell resists the point of the knife, they are still alive and kicking). Any shellfish that open easily are dead. As they decompose quickly, they must be thrown away.

On the Coast

The best plant that grows in abundance in salt marshes is samphire. The fragrant, fleshy leaves can be picked, then lightly steamed or boiled. The green flesh is then sucked off the inner fibrous stems. Samphire has a most delicate and delicious flavour, not unlike asparagus.

Seakale is often seen around our coasts, displaying its grey-green bouquets of foliage through great shoals of pebbles. The leaves are *not* eaten, but the stem is. If it is cultivated, the plants are blanched to give longer, whiter stems. If you find wild seakale, trim the roots and wash the stalks. It can be tied into bundles like asparagus, boiled for about 15 minutes and eaten hot or cold.

Seaweed can also be gathered, but as it requires lengthy preparation and cooking, this is probably one wild ingredient it is best to try in the packet.

Nuts

In October and November, near where I live, all the locals know where the sweet chestnut trees are, and their fruit is picked. One has to be quick and watch the trees, waiting for the fruit to fall. Sweet chestnuts that are cooked and eaten fresh have a special flavour. I boil them for 20 minutes, let them cook, nick their skins and peel them. Then I sauté them in butter, oil and garlic. They can also be roasted on an open fire. Mixed with cottage cheese and onions, they can be used as a sandwich filling. They can be added to ice cream, or glazed with honey or sugar and added to a pudding. If you get a good haul, sweet chestnuts can be used (after the initial boiling) in all manner of stuffings.

Hazelnuts are more difficult to find. They grow on shrubs twelve feet high in woods and hedgerows, but the squirrels tend to find them first. They become ripe sometime around September and can be cracked open and eaten raw. They can be chopped and added to puddings and ice cream or finely chopped and added to salads, which is probably the most practical way of using them for a picnic.

Fungi

In the autumn fungi can be abundant, but there are very strict rules for gathering them. Take two books on the subject along with you, or one book plus a reference chart with clear photographs and drawings. Check and double check every specimen you see. Never eat any fungi raw; some are toxic raw, but perfectly safe if cooked. Pick the specimens whole so that you can see both the stem and the bulbous part in the soil at the end of the stem. Read an account of each specimen picked, checking each point carefully.

Some fungi are difficult to identify, since your specimen may be at a different stage of development than that shown in the book. Any specimen you might have any doubts about, discard.

This advice is ultra-cautious, but it is best to be safe. Out of about 3,000 species of fungi found in the UK, about twenty are toxic. Some of these are so brilliantly coloured, they would be difficult to miss. Others can appear similar to some of the best edible species; there are no general rules. In France every chemist's shop displays coloured charts and every chemist will look over your collected specimens. It is a pity this is not done in this country, for we miss much because of our ignorance. I list below a few of the many delicious varieties of fungi. Most can be cooked by simply sautéing them in butter.

Field mushrooms. There are two varieties of field mushrooms. One is the wild version of cultivated mushrooms (agaricus campestris), and the other is a larger, shaggier version (agaricus vaporarius). They are easily identifiable by sight and smell.

Parasol mushrooms are usually found on grassy hillsides. Their size makes them quite easy to find. They should be picked young, when they have an excellent flavour.

Giant Puffball. Found in woods and meadows, these are the ultimate taste sensation in wild foods. They should be ivory in colour throughout with the outside skin perhaps paler. They should only be eaten when they are young and firm. They can be very large; twice as big as a football. They can be sliced like steaks and sautéed on both sides or grilled. They are, in my opinion, the best, most luxurious treat, and I wish someone would cultivate them.

Ceps, a favourite French fungi, grow here in abundance. They are easily identifiable and can be dried and stored.

Chanterelles, commonly found in woods, are another French favourite. They smell faintly of apricots when raw. When cooked, they have a slightly peppery taste with a delicate perfume. Their firm flesh requires longer cooking than other fungi.

Flowers

It is one of the greatest pleasures of summer to be able to make salads that include flowers as well as leaves. This can often be done on picnics. Even if the flowers are small, they look attractive and most are edible.

All herb flowers can be eaten. Study a reference book on the subject. The plants that have leaves that can be picked also have edible flowers.

Cowslips can also be eaten, but they have been over-picked. I would leave any specimen found to seed itself. There are several clumps of cowslips in my garden which I refuse to pick or eat.

It would be an impossible task to discuss each edible flower separately. Some have rather distinctive flavours. Nasturtium, for example, echoes the peppery taste of its leaves. It is a very dramatic flower for a salad, but an unlikely one to find growing wild. Some of the flowers you are likely to find are: wild violets and wild pansies, elder and hop flowers, chamomile, wild daisies, dog roses, primroses and wild geraniums. Poisonous flowers to avoid are the buttercup and foxglove.

Fruits

Blackberries are the first wild fruits to spring to mind, and how excellent they are, lightly cooked in their own juices with a little honey. They are especially good served hot over ice cream.

Sometimes one can find wild strawberries, and these are splendid eaten raw. They are very sweet and need little or nothing added to them in the way of cream of sugar.

In my neighbourhood, the bullace plum is picked in the autumn. This is not picnic fare, but a delicious sharp jam can be made using these wild plums. Other fruits to be picked for cooking at home, after the picnic, are rosehips, and sloes. The latter is famous for its use in gin; I prefer to make sloe vodka, or jam or jelly. Sloes have an intensity and depth of flavour which will astonish you if you have never tasted them before.

PICNICS

One of the most enjoyable aspects of summer eating is the picnic. The concept of a 'picnic', a meal taken in the open air for pleasure, or a meal to which each participant contributes a dish, is relatively recent. It is thought that the word originates from the French *pique-nique*, which in turn comes from two words: *piquer* – to pick or peck, and *nique* – a trifle.

It was the Victorians who made picnics popular. Obviously, for the fashion to catch on, the Queen had to endorse it, and she wrote fondly of picnics *à deux* with Albert in her diaries and letters. In her later years, she posed for the camera (and posterity) – a black butterball surrounded by family and gillies – at picnics of mammoth proportions, but dull ingredients. Our royal family still seem to build their alfresco meals around 'little corpses', or, as Princess Margaret puts it, 'that standby of the English, various cold meats'. We are told that the Duke of Edinburgh likes to barbecue steaks and sausages, while the Queen is apparently a dab hand at vinaigrette. However, Prince Charles has implied that he personally avoids meat.

Back in the nineteenth century, the expansion of the railways in the British Isles helped the picnic, for it became possible for the working man's family to go out for day excursions to the sea or countryside.

Abroad, the picnic was also an acceptable form of entertainment. In India, a large retinue of servants carried elaborate tableware and cutlery, not to mention crates of claret and champagne and hampers filled with cold carcasses and haunches of beef – a most undesirable diet for a hot climate. No wonder that so many of the ruling class suffered from high blood pressure and became so easily apoplectic.

Royal approval of overeating had its final personification in Edward VII. It was in the Edwardian era that picnics for the aristocracy seemed to burgeon in courses and grandeur.

The rest of us had to be more modest. My mother, a child of the Edwardian era, remembers picnics of egg sandwiches and cakes; both of these being a treat. When the family were by the sea, the picnic was augmented by winkles and cockles, and for dad, jellied eels.

Today the picnic is a flexible as well as a movable feast. The motor car has brought inaccessible places within our reach. We can now picnic on the land, on the sea and in the air. But we have learned that we are what we eat and that the same care should be taken regarding what we consume in the picnic diet as in our other meals.

There are myriad ways of eating out of doors. Lunching al fresco in your garden, where the food is brought ten yards from the kitchen, is a wholly different experience from eating on a barge on the Grand Union Canal. Where you enjoy your picnics and how many people are involved determines the level of formality and the food you eat; for example, a family meal in the garden is different from a buffet party for fifty. A barbecue in the garden is different from a barbecue on a beach in Spain. A picnic at Glyndebourne is different from one at Ascot or one on a ferry. But there are common factors to all good picnics. The food must be fresh and seasonal, delicious and enticing. Your picnic must be far superior to anyone else's. Strive for signs of pleasure, oohs and ahs of envy and appreciation. Picnic food must be well-packed, leak-proof and easy to carry. It must also be easy to eat, either with the fingers or with a fork. In terms of health-consciousness, it should be designed to agree with current nutritional thinking: it should not rely on any manufactured foods with chemical additives; it should be low in saturated fat, sugar and salt and high in fibre. If it seems that some recipes in this book do not comply with these parameters, it is simply because a picnic is a small part of the total balanced diet. Therefore, a dish high in saturated fat eaten on Sunday should, one hopes, be counterbalanced throughout the week with dishes that are low in saturated fat.

The following pages contain no recipes for meat or fowl. I believe that factory-farmed flesh is a possible health hazard. The feed of these animals contains a collection of additives, antibiotics and growth hormones of which a residue remains in the carcass, which may affect the consumer. Because the animals get little or no exercise – many can only move a few inches in their lifetime as they are chained into confined spaces – the weight put on turns to fat, not muscle. This is the saturated fat that can lead to heart attacks. There is a growing suspicion that broiler chickens now also have an inclination towards heart disease, for their diet and confined living space are destined to provoke the diseases of the First World – the citizens of which live sedentary lives and consume too much protein. These animals have a wretched existence. Even if there were no health hazards regarding the consumption of their flesh, I would hope that civilized societies would still reject eating them. Intensive factory farming is patently against the welfare of farm animals.

Eliminating meat and poultry from the diet removes many staple picnic foods. It is my intention to prove that your picnic will be far more delicious and imaginative without these foods and that the scope of dishes can grow rather than diminish. Should you enquire why this is, I think the reason is that a barrier in the mind is pulled away. The imagination then creates many new vegetable and fish dishes. Such a quest brings surprises and rewards; some of these are in the following pages.

Although I feel strongly about avoiding meat and poultry and feel especially passionate about factory-farmed animals and birds, I do not think it worth spending a lot of energy on the minutiae of such a stand. I am ambivalent about cheese made from animal rennet, but I don't think I should feel guilty about using it. It is difficult, if not impossible, in a modern society, to eschew all animal products. The main principle is what is important. The details will take care of themselves.

These are my views, and now that I have voiced them, there is no point in going on *ad nauseam*. Instead, I shall get on with how to enhance the pleasures of picnics.

1

PLANNING A PICNIC

EQUIPMENT

As with everything else, equipment can be improvised, but picnics are easier to enjoy if you have a few basics. I tend to want picnics, however simple, to have a certain elegance. The right equipment offers a semblance of panache.

A proper picnic hamper is not essential, but it is pleasant to have. One can buy hampers complete with cutlery and plates, but they are usually rather tasteless. It is better by far to buy an empty basket and use your own cutlery and china. (When you are feeling flush, you can order a hamper crammed with delicacies, eat the goodies, then use the basket.) You can, of course, use an ordinary shopping basket, or even a suitcase. Improvisation, as I've said above, consists of infinite possibilities.

There is one piece of equipment that is essential if one wants cold drinks and cool food – a cool box. They come in many sizes, complete with trays of dry ice, that will stay cold for twelve hours. The largest size can masquerade as a small refrigerator. it can be stood up in the back of a car or in a tent and used as a cold store cupboard. If picnics appeal to you, it might be worthwhile investing in a couple of cool boxes. They also come in handy at home to cool drinks for parties.

There are also insulated cool bags which zip up. My experience with these has been unhappy. They have had short lives, with seams coming undone, insulation tearing and zips breaking. But they are undeniably useful, so choose one with a sound guarantee and send it back if it fails to work.

There is a huge range of plastic food storage containers on the market that are ideal for packing food for a picnic. Choose rigid containers made of sturdy materials with tightly fitting lids. Since not all soups and sauces require vacuum flasks to keep them either hot or cold, you might also find it convenient to buy plastic jars with lids and pouring spouts. Ideally, you should buy containers in a size and shape that will fit together like a jigsaw puzzle, leaving no gaps when it comes to the final packing.

China and cutlery are a matter of personal preference, Barbara Cartland, in her advice to lovers on picnics, suggests disposable plates and cutlery, as cleaning up dirty plates is 'unromantic'. I think that eating a meal off a paper plate with a plastic fork is the 'the pits'. I unequivocally loathe disposable cutlery and plates; it is all part of our disposable society. Good food needs a good setting to make it most appealing, but it needn't be bone china. I have no objection to nature's disposable plates found *in situ*. The best curry I ever had was presented on a banana leaf in Singapore. Though you are unlikely to find banana leaves outside the tropics, there are many other leaves that will make handsome plates – some you can even take with you from home. Cos lettuce leaves are excellent, if the stems are sliced so that they are pliable. So are cabbage leaves and Swiss chard. This may seem a bit affected, but do try it occasionally; think how fragrant wild strawberries will be presented on their own leaf, or a bunch of succulent grapes on a vine leaf. I have even used plates made from bark and wood found on the picnic site.

For my picnic, I would choose Victorian or Edwardian china. No matter if little matches; one can still pick up pretty dishes and plates fairly cheaply. It would not be difficult to collect odd pieces of china and keep them just for picnics.

All of the above is totally unfeasible if the planned picnic is to be packed in haversacks and taken on one's back when climbing or trekking. In these circumstances, it is best to choose lightweight bags, containers and cutlery and use your lap for a plate. (Do take one all-purpose clasp knife with several blades.) You can still add a little style to this sort of picnic by choosing a really breathtaking site and using the flowers and leaves you find as part of the event.

FORWARD PLANNING

Well in advance of the picnic, make a list. Decide how you are going to get to the picnic site, what activities you will participate in and what you would like to eat. In other words, think *everything* through as thoroughly as you can. Otherwise, the inevitable will happen and a vital object will be missing, such as a corkscrew, tin opener or matches. Odd things come in handy at picnics – a length of string or a torch, perhaps. A damp cloth in a plastic bag is useful for wiping childrens' faces and hands, and a roll of paper towels can be utilized to clean plates and keep containers from rattling against each other. Plastic rubbish bags will facilitate the disposal of debris, and a plastic ground sheet can be a great boon spread beneath the travelling rug. (For several years I used a threadbare Persian carpet as a travelling rug: it looked attractive and was comfortable to sit on.) A few cushions also help – even if they are inflatable ones – and lightweight folding chairs. However, these items are contingent upon a car to carry them, which can be parked near the site. It all depends on how simple you want your picnic to be and whether children or older people are present.

PACKING THE PICNIC

Whatever type of picnic you choose, sensible packing is a necessity. Otherwise, objects will rattle during the journey, food may leak or spill and china may possibly break. Some tips I have found useful are:

1. Wrap food well. Aluminium foil is a good material, because food will not sweat through it, it keeps sandwiches from becoming soggy and prevents items stowed in warm places (like car boots) from becoming too hot. Cling film is a good wrapping for those items that are not easily squashed.
2. If your picnic site is a long car journey away, freeze your sandwiches and pack just before you depart. They will defrost en route and taste freshly made on your arrival.
3. Pies, tarts and tartlets should first be wrapped in aluminium foil, then put into a tightly sealed plastic container to be transported.
4. Pasties, tartlets and turnovers or any food totally enclosed in pastry is easier to eat with the fingers or one piece of cutlery than a wedge of pie from which the filling might ooze.

5.   Pack items as tightly together as possible. Cushion hard or breakable objects with travelling rugs, towels or crumpled paper.
6.   Use empty plastic tubs with tightly fitting lids to pack salads, sauces, desserts, etc.

WHAT TO DRINK?

This can be a vexing question because of the weight of bottles and the significance of what is inside. However, it is worthwhile hauling a few bottles for the pleasure they contain. I save partitioned cardboard boxes from wine merchants to transport bottles to picnics. They will also carry fruit juice and soft drinks safely as well as vacuum flasks.

Chilled white wine can be transported in a cool box or bag. If you are having your picnic near water, the traditional method for chilling wine is to find a spot in the river or sea and wedge the bottle between rocks or secure it with string. This always strikes me as a dangerous ploy, but I have never lost a bottle in thirty years. What is more, the wine is always beautifully cool.

Good red wines have to be carefully packed, carried and handled to avoid disturbing the sediment. But for most picnics, heavy wines are unsuitable; it is not really a good idea for picnickers to become so lethargic that they are plunged into a stupor. Lighter red wines can sometimes be drunk cool and will taste better that way. Picnics call for the unusual. I once had a dry sparkling red wine which was delicious – drunk cool, of course.

Mulled wine can be taken in a vacuum flask or prepared on the spot over a campfire.

Other refreshing drinks are a dash of ginger wine with beer (Shandy Gaff), half beer and half lemonade (plain Shandy), Guinness and champagne (Black Velvet), champagne and orange juice (Bucks Fizz), or champagne and peach juice (Mimosa). A dry sparkling white wine can be substituted for champagne in these mixtures. Other wine-based drinks are: Kir, which is made by adding a dash or more of Crème de Cassis (blackcurrant liqueur) to a glass of dry white wine; and Kir Royale, the same as Kir only with champagne. A different, but just as delicious drink can be made by substituting Framboise (raspberry liqueur) for the cassis or the current French favourite – myrtle sauvage. You can also try Sangria, a refreshing mixture of light red wine, orange and lemon juice and cut-up fresh fruit.

If you wish to start the picnic meal with an aperitif, a long cocktail like a Tom Collins might be just the thing. Mix three parts gin with one part lemon or lime juice. Add a little castor sugar and shake with crushed ice, then top up with six parts soda water. Vodka or white rum can be substituted for the gin if you prefer. Another very popular aperitif is a Pimms. You can find these ready-mixed; all you have to add is ice, lemonade, lemon or orange slices plus borage flowers. Better still, you might find herb flowers growing wild at your picnic site.

Fruit juices are available in square cartons which pack easily. Mineral waters come in plastic bottles and there are now numerous fruit essences, squashes and syrups that are pure and additive-free. Do read the labels with care. If weight is a consideration and there is a supply of fresh water at the picnic site, it might be a good idea to take a can of concentrated fruit juice and an empty plastic jug and stirrer.

Yogurt drinks are particularly refreshing in summer if they are kept really cool in a vacuum flask. Mix them in the proportion of half yogurt to half water. Flavour either with a pinch of salt or a little honey and blend together thoroughly. A richer drink can be made with half yogurt and half soya milk or skimmed milk (some people do not like the nutty taste of soya). A delicious yogurt fruit drink can be made by adding a few spoonsful of fruit essence or crushed soft fruit to half yogurt and half skimmed milk, water or soya milk. For a fruit drink that is rich enough to be called dessert, use half yogurt and half single cream. Or omit the fruit and add a couple of ounces (60g) grated plain chocolate and a tablespoonful of brown sugar.

Plain fruit juice becomes even nicer when you add crushed soft fruit and blend thoroughly. It is then similar to a fruit cup, and any combination of summer fruit and juice is delicious. You can pep up this drink by adding a little dry white wine or sherry. This sort of drink is best combined at the picnic site, because fruit, once peeled, easily oxidizes and will look unappetizing. There is also something pleasurable about preparing food and drink in the open air.

Tea or coffee taste better if they are brewed just before drinking. I am a coffee drinker and find that a simple espresso maker and small Calor gas burner can easily be packed in the car to make fresh black coffee for the end of the meal. Tea can be made using the same method, using tea bags. While some tea drinkers are such purists that they cannot bear the thought of tea bags, most people find them acceptable. Iced tea or coffee tastes marvellous in warm climes or in the summer – but remember to brew these beverages extra strong as they will be diluted by the ice (unless you are clever and make ice cubes out of brewed coffee or tea beforehand).

2

SPECIAL OCCASION PICNICS

A Glyndebourne Picnic
Mediterranean Beach Picnic
Mountain Climb
A Cold Day at the Races
A Buffet in the Garden
Movable Feasts

A GLYNDEBOURNE PICNIC

I suppose it was in the early sixties when I first went to a Glyndebourne opera. It was *L'Incoronazione di Poppea*, and I remember that I experienced as much pleasure in planning and cooking the meal we took with us as I did in seeing the opera.

There is nothing quite like having a picnic in the gardens of Glyndebourne, sitting on the lawn beside wide herbaceous borders of pure colour. It is a grand occasion for which evening dress, or at least something suitably striking, is worn, and it seems to me that the picnic ought to be grand as well. I once saw someone who had a white damask tablecloth and silver candelabra, which I found deliciously amusing. Another time, I heard that the opera chorus, with nothing to do at the beginning of an opera, got so bored that they entertained themselves by changing all the picnic hampers around.

This meal for four to six people has been designed to be eaten from a hamper with table linen, real china and proper cutlery. To include lobster in the menu may seem extravagant, but lobster is so rich and packed with protein, that you need a very small amount per person — two large lobsters or three small ones will be sufficient for the entire party. Champagne seems to be *de rigueur* at Glyndebourne. Pink champagne looks so pretty that I have chosen it to begin the meal. The best of the fruits and vegetables are in season during the summer, so why not take advantage of them?

MENU for 4-6 PEOPLE

Asparagus Croustades
Lobster Salad *or* Indonesian Vegetable Stew
Fresh Green Pea Moulds
Millet Pilaf
Celery Loaf
Salad Elona

Pink Champagne
Pouilly Fumé

ASPARAGUS CROUSTADES

Preparation time: 10 minutes
Cooking time: 20 minutes

IMPERIAL (METRIC)
8 sheets filo pastry (see note below)
3 tablespoonsful sunflower oil
2 lb (900g) asparagus
1 oz (30g) butter, melted
2 eggs, separated
Sea salt and freshly ground black
   pepper

AMERICAN
8 sheets filo pastry (see note below)
3 tablespoonsful sunflower oil
2 lb asparagus
2 tablespoonsful butter, melted
2 eggs, separated
Sea salt and freshly ground black
   pepper

1. Preheat the oven to 400°F/200°C (Gas Mark 6). Butter or oil 4–6 individual Yorkshire pudding tins.
2. Place the filo pastry in one stack. Using a saucer as a guide, cut out rounds. (Note: if you are preparing this recipe for 6, you will need additional filo pastry, as each croustade will consist of 8 circles of pastry.)
3. Brush each circle of pastry with a little oil. Place them, leaf by leaf, in each tin so that they overlap, like petals.
4. Place a few ceramic beans in the bottom of each tin and bake blind for 15–18 minutes or until the pastry is crisp and golden-brown. Remove from the oven and allow to cool.
5. Meanwhile, trim the asparagus and poach in a little salted water for 8 minutes. Remove from the heat and drain. Slice off the tips and set aside; cut off any fibrous stalks and discard.
6. Blend the asparagus stalks in an electric blender with the butter and egg yolks. Season to taste. Whisk the egg whites until stiff and fold into the purée.
7. Remove the ceramic beans from the croustades and fill with the purée. Garnish with the reserved asparagus tips.

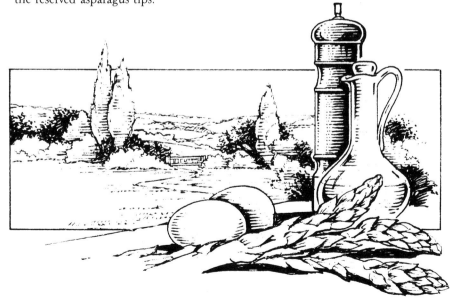

LOBSTER SALAD

Preparation time: 20–30 minutes

IMPERIAL (METRIC)
1 ripe avocado
¼ pint (140ml) soured cream
1 teaspoonful green peppercorns
Sea salt and freshly ground black
   pepper
2 large or *3 small cooked lobsters*
1 bunch spring onions, finely
   chopped
3 tablespoonsful finely chopped
   parsley

AMERICAN
1 ripe avocado
⅔ cup sour cream
1 teaspoonful green peppercorns
Sea salt and freshly ground black
   pepper
2 large or *3 small cooked lobsters*
1 bunch scallions, finely chopped

3 tablespoonsful finely chopped
   parsley

1. First make the sauce. Stone the avocado and scoop the flesh into a blender container. Add the soured cream, green peppercorns and seasoning and blend to a smooth purée.
2. Place each lobster on its back on a work surface and slice in half down the centre. Remove the small, gritty pouch at the mouth and the dark green thread that runs down the tail and discard. Everything else (except the shell) can be eaten. The green liver (tomalley) is particularly delicious and will enrich the sauce. The coral also adds colour and flavour.
3. Slice the flesh from the lobster bodies into a bowl. Add the lobster tails, which you have cut into chunks. Crack the claws, remove the flesh and add to the bowl. Mix together with the avocado sauce and the spring onions.
4. Either serve from a glass bowl sprinkled with parsley or, better still, use half lobster shells as serving dishes. Pile the salad into the shells, sprinkle with parsley and wrap with cling film.

INDONESIAN VEGETABLE STEW

Preparation time: 35 minutes
Cooking time: 2 hours

IMPERIAL (METRIC)	AMERICAN
3 tablespoonsful olive oil	*3 tablespoonsful olive oil*
1 teaspoonful mustard seeds	*1 teaspoonful mustard seeds*
1 teaspoonful ground turmeric	*1 teaspoonful ground turmeric*
1 teaspoonful fenugreek	*1 teaspoonful fenugreek*
1 teaspoonful cumin seeds	*1 teaspoonful cumin seeds*
2 oz (55g) root ginger, peeled and thinly sliced	*½ cup peeled and thinly sliced ginger root*
3 cloves garlic, thinly sliced	*3 cloves garlic, thinly sliced*
2 onions, thinly sliced	*2 onions, thinly sliced*
2 celeriac roots, peeled and diced	*2 celeriac roots, peeled and diced*
1½ lb (680g) new potatoes, sliced	*1½ lb new potatoes, sliced*
½ lb (225g) mushrooms, sliced	*½ lb mushrooms, sliced*
1 lb (455g) baby carrots, cut into sticks	*1 lb baby carrots, cut into sticks*
1 lb (455g) baby courgettes, cut into sticks	*1 lb baby zucchini, cut into sticks*
2 oz (55g) creamed coconut, grated	*½ cup grated creamed coconut*
¼ pint (140ml) single cream	*⅔ cup light cream*
Sea salt	*Sea salt*

1. Heat the oil in a large saucepan over low heat. Add the mustard seeds, turmeric, fenugreek, cumin, ginger and garlic and sauté for a few minutes, or until the mustard seeds pop.
2. Add the onions, celeriac, potatoes, mushrooms, carrots and courgettes and enough water to cover the vegetables by 2 inches (5cm). Bring to the boil and simmer for 20 minutes. Add the creamed coconut and stir well. Simmer for a further 2 minutes. Remove from the heat and add the cream. Season with sea salt to taste. Allow to cool.
3. Place the stew in a serving dish and chill in the refrigerator for about 2 hours.

FRESH GREEN PEA MOULDS

Preparation time:	20 minutes
Cooking time:	5–10 minutes
Baking time:	20 minutes

IMPERIAL (METRIC)
1½–2 lb (680–900g) garden peas in their pods
Sprig of fresh mint
3 eggs
1 oz (30g) butter, softened
¼ pint (140ml) fromage frais or Greek yogurt
Sea salt and freshly ground black pepper

AMERICAN
1½–2 lb garden peas in their pods
Sprig of fresh mint
3 eggs
2 tablespoonsful butter, softened
⅔ cup fromage frais or Greek yogurt
Sea salt and freshly ground black pepper

1. Preheat the oven to 400°F/200°C (Gas Mark 6). Butter 4–6 small ramekins.
2. Pod the peas, place in a medium-sized saucepan and cook with the mint in a little boiling, salted water for 5–10 minutes, until just tender. Drain well and place the peas in a blender container. Add the eggs, butter, fromage frais or yogurt and a little seasoning. Blend to a purée.
3. Pour the purée into the buttered ramekins to about ½ inch (1.25cm) from the tops of the moulds. Place in a bain-marie or baking dish filled with hot water, cover with buttered greaseproof paper and bake for 20 minutes, or until the mixture has just risen to the tops of the moulds.
4. Remove from the oven, set aside to cool, then unmould.

Opposite: Crab and Courgette Terrine (page 82).
Overleaf: A Glyndebourne Picnic (pages 20 to 26).

MILLET PILAF

Preparation time: minimal
Cooking time: 20 minutes

IMPERIAL (METRIC)
6 oz (170g) millet
1 red pepper, deseeded and finely chopped
1 green pepper, deseeded and finely chopped
Generous handful of mint, finely chopped
Zest and juice of 1 lemon
2 cloves garlic, crushed
2 tablespoonsful olive oil
Sea salt and freshly ground black pepper

AMERICAN
1 scant cup millet
1 red pepper, seeded and finely chopped
1 green pepper, seeded and finely chopped
Generous handful of mint, finely chopped
Zest and juice of 1 lemon
2 cloves garlic, crushed
2 tablespoonsful olive oil
Sea salt and freshly ground black pepper

1. Place the millet in a measuring jug to note its volume, then tip into a medium-sized saucepan. Cover with 2½ times its volume of water and bring to the boil. Reduce the heat and simmer for 20 minutes, or until tender. Drain in a colander.
2. In a bowl, mix together the peppers with the mint. While it is still hot, add the drained millet, then add the lemon zest and juice, garlic, olive oil, salt and pepper. Mix thoroughly.
3. Spoon the millet mixture into a container with a tightly fitting lid and refrigerate until needed.

Opposite: Vegetable Pie (page 103).

CELERY LOAF

Preparation time:	15 minutes
Rising time:	45 minutes–1¾ hours, depending on type of yeast used
Baking time:	40 minutes

IMPERIAL (METRIC)
1 lb (455g) strong unbleached white
  bread flour
Pinch of sea salt
1 teaspoonful celery salt
1 tablespoonful celery seed
1 sachet micronized yeast
2 tablespoonsful olive oil
½ pint (285ml) warm water

AMERICAN
4 cups unbleached white bread flour
Pinch of sea salt
1 teaspoonful celery salt
1 tablespoonful celery seed
1 package active dry yeast and
  1 teaspoonful sugar dissolved in ¼
  cup tepid water
2 tablespoonsful olive oil
1 cup warm water

1. Read the general instructions for home baking on page 137.
2. Sift the flour into a bowl, add the micronized yeast, sea salt, celery salt and celery seed and mix thoroughly.
3. Add the oil and water (and dry yeast mixture, if using), mix and knead for 5–8 minutes, until the dough is elastic. Form into a ball, place back into the bowl, cover and allow to rise in a warm place, free from draughts, for 1 hour, until double in bulk.
4. Grease a 1½ lb (680g) bread tin, fit the dough into the tin and leave to rise to the top of the tin about 45 minutes.
5. Preheat the oven to 425°F/220°C (Gas Mark 7).
6. Bake the bread for 40 minutes. Test to see that it is done by tapping the bottom of the loaf. If it sounds hollow, remove from the oven and cool on a wire rack. If not, return to the oven for another 4 or 5 minutes.

SALAD ELONA

Preparation time:	5 minutes

IMPERIAL (METRIC)
1 large cucumber
1 punnet strawberries
3 fl oz (90ml) dry white wine
Freshly ground black pepper

AMERICAN
2 cucumbers
1 carton strawberries
3 fl oz dry white wine
Freshly ground black pepper

1. Scrape the skin of the cucumber away with a fork in stripes. Slice the cucumber thinly and wrap in cling film until it is time for the salad to be served, as it is quickly assembled on the site.
2. When ready to serve, spread the cucumber slices out on a shallow plate. Hull the strawberries and slice in half. Arrange over the cucumber. Pour the wine over and grind the pepper generously over the salad.

MEDITERRANEAN BEACH PICNIC

I suppose I have had more picnics on Mediterranean beaches than anywhere else in the world, and it is still one of my most intense pleasures. If you can manage to obtain a bottle of local wine and keep it cool, all the better. This picnic is based on foods you might find in any Mediterranean country in the summer.

MENU for 4-6 PEOPLE

Stuffed Globe Artichokes
Espadon en Croûte (Swordfish baked in Pastry)
   or Fungi en Croûte (Mushrooms baked in Pastry)
Tomato and Basil Salad
Potato and Pepper Salad
Local cheese and bread
Fresh fruits

To drink:
one of
the good
local wines

STUFFED GLOBE ARTICHOKES

Preparation time: 45 minutes
Cooking time: 45 minutes

IMPERIAL (METRIC)
4–6 large globe artichokes
1 lb (455g) broad beans in their pods
Zest and juice of 1 lemon or *lime*
2 small onions, thinly sliced
3 cloves garlic, crushed
¼ pint (140ml) fromage frais or
  Greek yogurt

AMERICAN
4–6 large globe artichokes
1 lb fava beans in their pods
Zest and juice of 1 lemon or *lime*
2 small onions, thinly sliced
3 cloves garlic, crushed
⅔ cup fromage frais or *Greek yogurt*

1. Trim the artichokes by slicing the tips off the leaves and cutting the bases so that they will stand upright. Place in a large saucepan, cover with water and bring to the boil. Boil for 40–45 minutes. Drain and set aside to cool.
2. Meanwhile, pod the beans and slip off the outer skins. Boil for 2–3 minutes in very little lightly salted water until tender, then drain and set aside to cool.
3. Chop the beans coarsely and place in a bowl with the lemon or lime zest and juice, onions, garlic and fromage frais or yogurt. Mix thoroughly, then chill in the refrigerator.
4. When the artichokes are cooked, remove the inner leaves, leaving a firm wall of outer leaves. Dig out the choke with a sharp, pointed spoon and discard.
5. Just before you pack the picnic hamper, fill the artichokes with the broad bean mixture and wrap and pack securely.

ESPADON EN CROÛTE (Swordfish baked in Pastry)

Preparation time: 20 minutes
Baking time: 50 minutes

IMPERIAL (METRIC)
2½–3 lb (1.1–1.4kg) swordfish steak
  in one piece
1 bunch fresh dillweed or *fennel*
2 oz (55g) butter, softened
Sea salt and freshly ground black
  pepper
½ lb (225g) frozen puff pastry,
  defrosted

AMERICAN
2½–3 lb swordfish steak in one piece
1 bunch fresh dill or *fennel*
4 tablespoonsful butter, softened
Sea salt and freshly ground black
  pepper
8 oz frozen puff pastry, defrosted

1. Preheat the oven to 425°F/220°C (Gas Mark 7). Grease a baking sheet.
2. Place the swordfish on a firm surface and remove the black skin and centre bone (which is easily accomplished with a sharp knife by cutting around it).
3. Chop the dillweed or fennel finely and mix with the butter in a small bowl. Add seasoning to taste and fill the cavity of the fish with most of the herb butter. Spread the remaining herb butter on the top and bottom of the fish.
4. Roll out the pastry thinly to a size that will completely enclose the fish. Place the fish on the pastry and wrap up, pinching the ends together to seal.

5. Place the pastry-wrapped fish on the baking sheet seam-side down and bake for 20 minutes. Reduce the oven temperature to 375°F/190°C (Gas Mark 5) and bake for a further 30 minutes. Remove from the oven and allow to cool.
6. To serve, cut in ½-inch (1.25cm) slices.

FUNGI EN CROÛTE (Mushrooms baked in Pastry)

Soaking time: 30 minutes
Cooking time: 45 minutes
Baking time: 20 hours

IMPERIAL (METRIC)
¼ oz (7g) dried Italian fungi (porcini mushrooms)
¼ pint (140ml) dry white wine
¼ pint (140ml) vegetable stock
1 lb (455g) celeriac root, peeled, cooked and diced
Generous handful of parsley, finely chopped
Sea salt and freshly ground black pepper
½ lb (225g) frozen puff pastry, defrosted

AMERICAN
½ cup dried wild mushrooms, preferably porcini
⅔ cup dry white wine
⅔ cup vegetable stock
1 lb celeriac, pared, cooked and diced
Generous handful of parsley, finely chopped
Sea salt and freshly ground black pepper
8 oz frozen puff pastry, defrosted

1. Place the fungi in a small jug and pour in the wine and stock. Allow to soak for 30 minutes.
2. Place the mushroom mixture in a medium-sized saucepan and bring to the boil over moderate heat. Add the celeriac and simmer gently for 15 minutes. Watch carefully to see that the mixture does not dry out; if necessary, add more vegetable stock. Remove from the heat.
3. Add the parsley and seasoning to the mushroom and celeriac mixture.
4. Preheat the oven to 425°F/220°C (Gas Mark 7).
5. Roll out the pastry thinly into a circle. Pile the filling in the centre and fold over the pastry like a giant pasty. Seal the edges well.
6. Place the croûte on a baking sheet and bake for 20 minutes, or until golden-brown. Remove from the oven and set aside to cool.

TOMATO AND BASIL SALAD

I think this salad is best assembled on the beach, so if possible, pack a chopping board and sharp knife, but prepare the dressing in advance and pour into a container with a tightly fitting lid.

Preparation time: minimal

IMPERIAL (METRIC)
Large bunch of basil
2 cloves garlic, crushed
1 tablespoonful lemon juice
3 tablespoonsful olive oil
Sea salt and freshly ground black
  pepper
1½ lb (680g) Marmande (very large)
  tomatoes

AMERICAN
Large bunch of basil
2 cloves garlic, crushed
1 tablespoonful lemon juice
3 tablespoonsful olive oil
Sea salt and freshly ground black
  pepper
1½ lb Marmande (very large)
  tomatoes

1. Chop the basil finely.
2. In a small bowl, mix together the garlic, lemon juice and olive oil thoroughly. Season to taste and stir in the chopped basil.
3. Just before serving, coarsely slice the tomatoes crossways. Place a few slices on each plate and cover with the dressing.

POTATO AND PEPPER SALAD

Preparation time: 15 minutes
Cooking time: 20 minutes

IMPERIAL (METRIC)
1½ lb (680g) new potatoes
2 green peppers, deseeded and thinly
  sliced
1 onion, thinly sliced
Generous handful of mint, finely
  chopped
3 tablespoonsful olive oil
1 tablespoonful white wine vinegar
Sea salt and freshly ground black
  pepper

AMERICAN
1½ lb new potatoes
2 green peppers, seeded and thinly
  sliced
1 onion, thinly sliced
Generous handful of mint, finely
  chopped
3 tablespoonsful olive oil
1 tablespoonful white wine vinegar
Sea salt and freshly ground black
  pepper

1. Scrub the potatoes well, but do not peel. Place in a saucepan of lightly salted water and boil for 15–20 minutes, until tender. Remove from the heat and drain well.
2. Slice the potatoes coarsely. Place in a bowl with the remaining ingredients and toss and mix thoroughly while the potatoes are still warm. Set aside to cool, then cover with cling film.

Local cheese and fresh fruit

The great delight of being abroad is to experiment with unknown local cheeses and local fruits and vegetables, so I cannot think of a more perfect way of finishing this meal than by buying a variety of local cheese and local bread. Also, in the height of summer, the local fruits can be so good that it would be pointless to eat them any other way than as they come off the tree. Do wash them well before packing. (I never mind having my fruit washed in the sea, but do take care that it is not in a part of the Mediterranean that is polluted.) If you are concerned about the water, wash the fruit in bottled water.

A MOUNTAIN CLIMB

When choosing food for a picnic on a walking tour, hike or mountain climb, select your menu carefully.

Because you will be expending a lot of energy, you will need food that is rich in carbohydrates, but not too heavy to carry. Fragile food is not a good idea, since in the rough and tumble of the day, nothing is worse than soggy sandwiches that will fall apart in your hands, leaving you holding the crusts.

Whatever you choose, make sure that it is compact, will hold together when cut and is well packed in lightweight but sturdy plastic boxes that will hold their contents snugly. (If food shifts around inside its packing, it will fall apart.) Another problem is what to drink — nobody would opt to haul heavy bottles of wine up the side of a mountain. As I have imagined the weather to be fairly cold, I think a strong, hot drink carried in a vacuum flask is the very thing and spiced, buttered rum will warm the heart as well as the body.

Pastry, sandwiches and pasta may appear to be a bit on the heavy side, but the roulades are no ordinary sandwiches and the pastry and pasta are not at all heavy. The dessert might have a tendency to collapse, but if you wrap the pear halves individually in cling film and then pack them snugly into a box, this should not be a problem.

Other useful, lightweight items to pack might be cups for fresh spring water to slake your thirst.

MENU for 4-6 PEOPLE

Anchovy and Parsley Cheese Roulades *or*
   Avocado and Cheese Roulades
Spiced Fish and Vegetable Pie *or*
   Spiced Vegetable Pie
Pasta Salad
Green Leaf Salad
Pears Stuffed with Stilton

Hot Buttered Rum

Fresh spring water

ANCHOVY AND PARSLEY CHEESE ROULADES

Preparation time: 15 minutes
Chilling time: 2 hours

IMPERIAL (METRIC)
2 tins anchovies
2 oz (55g) butter, softened
4 oz (115g) cottage cheese
Generous handful of parsley, finely
  chopped
Sea salt and freshly ground black
  pepper
1 small wholemeal loaf

AMERICAN
2 tins anchovies
4 tablespoonsful butter, softened
½ cup cottage cheese
Generous handful of parsley, finely
  chopped
Sea salt and freshly ground black
  pepper
1 small wholewheat bread

1. Drain the oil from the anchovies, place them in a bowl and mash into a paste. In another bowl, mix the butter, cheese and parsley and blend thoroughly. Season to taste.
2. Remove the crusts from the bread, then slice lengthways, starting at the bottom. Spread each slice with a portion of the parsley-cheese filling. Cover with a portion of anchovy paste. Carefully roll up each slice into a neat cylinder. Chill in the refrigerator for at least 2 hours.
3. Remove the roulades from the refrigerator just before leaving for the picnic and slice crossways so that each slice is like a Catherine wheel.

AVOCADO AND CHEESE ROULADES

Preparation time: 15 minutes
Chilling time: 2 hours

IMPERIAL (METRIC)
4 oz (115g) cottage cheese
1 bunch spring onions, thinly sliced
1 ripe avocado
Sea salt and freshly ground black
  pepper
1 small wholemeal loaf

AMERICAN
½ cup cottage cheese
1 bunch scallions, thinly sliced
1 ripe avocado
Sea salt and freshly ground black
  pepper
1 small wholewheat bread

1. Spoon the cottage cheese into a bowl and add the spring onions.
2. Peel and stone the avocado. Dice the flesh and mix into the cheese mixture. Season with salt and plenty of freshly ground black pepper.
3. Remove the crusts from the bread, then slice lengthways, starting at the bottom. Spread each slice with a portion of the avocado mixture. Carefully roll up each slice into a neat cylinder. Chill in the refrigerator for at least 2 hours.
4. Remove the roulades from the refrigerator just before leaving for the picnic and slice crossways so that each slice is like a Catherine wheel.

SPICED FISH AND VEGETABLE PIE

You will need a quiche dish approximately 8 inches (20cm) in diameter and 1½ inches (4cm) deep.

Preparation time: 10 minutes
Cooking time: 25 minutes
Baking time: 40 minutes

IMPERIAL (METRIC)	AMERICAN
2 tablespoonsful sunflower oil	*2 tablespoonsful sunflower oil*
2 tablespoonsful mustard seeds	*2 tablespoonsful mustard seeds*
1 oz (30g) root ginger, peeled and thinly sliced	*¼ cup thinly sliced, pared ginger root*
1 teaspoonful ground turmeric	*1 teaspoonful ground turmeric*
1 teaspoonful fenugreek	*1 teaspoonful fenugreek*
1 lb (455g) dogfish (rock salmon), skinned and filleted	*1 lb halibut, skinned and filleted*
½ lb (225g) potatoes, peeled and diced	*½ lb potatoes, peeled and diced*
½ lb (225g) mushrooms, sliced	*½ lb mushrooms, sliced*
¼ pint (140ml) water	*⅔ cup water*
Sea salt and freshly ground black pepper	*Sea salt and freshly ground black pepper*
½ lb (225g) frozen puff pastry, defrosted	*8 oz frozen puff pastry, defrosted*
1 egg, beaten	*1 egg, beaten*

1. Heat the oil in a medium-sized saucepan over low heat. Add the mustard seeds, ginger, turmeric and fenugreek. Sauté until the mustard seeds begin to pop, about 5 minutes, then add the fish, potatoes and mushrooms. Heat to simmering, then give the mixture a good stir. Pour in the water. Season to taste and cook over very low heat for 15 minutes.
2. Meanwhile, preheat the oven to 425°F/220°C (Gas Mark 7). Grease the quiche tin. Roll out two-thirds of the pastry and fit into the tin, leaving enough pastry at the top edge to form a good seal with the lid.
3. When the fish mixture is cooked, remove from the heat and allow to cool slightly. Pour the filling into the tin and level the top. Roll out the remaining pastry and place over the pie, pinching the top and bottom crusts together to seal. Brush the top with beaten egg.
4. Place the pie on a baking sheet and bake for 40 minutes, or until the pie has risen and the top is golden-brown. Remove from the oven and allow to cool.
5. Pack the pie in its tin. To serve, unmould and slice when you have reached the picnic site.

SPICED VEGETABLE PIE

You will need a quiche dish approximately 8 inches (20cm) in diameter and 1½ inches (4cm) deep.

Preparation time: 10 minutes
Cooking time: 25 minutes
Baking time: 40 minutes

IMPERIAL (METRIC)
2 tablespoonsful sunflower oil
1 tablespoonful mustard seeds
1 oz (30g) root ginger, peeled and
  thinly sliced
1 teaspoonful ground turmeric
1 teaspoonful fenugreek
½ lb (225g) potatoes, peeled and
  diced
½ lb (225g) mushrooms, sliced
4 oz (115g) carrots, trimmed and
  chopped
4 oz (115g) courgettes, trimmed and
  chopped
¼ pint (140ml) water
Sea salt and freshly ground black
  pepper
½ lb (225g) frozen puff pastry,
  defrosted
1 egg, beaten

AMERICAN
2 tablespoonsful sunflower oil
1 tablespoonful mustard seeds
¼ cup thinly sliced, pared ginger root
1 teaspoonful ground turmeric
1 teaspoonful fenugreek
½ lb potatoes, peeled and diced
½ lb mushrooms, sliced
¼ lb carrots, trimmed and chopped
¼ lb zucchini, trimmed and chopped
⅔ cup water
Sea salt and freshly ground black
  pepper
8 oz frozen puff pastry, defrosted
1 egg, beaten

1. Heat the oil in a medium-sized saucepan over low heat. Add the mustard seeds, ginger, turmeric and fenugreek. Sauté until the mustard seeds begin to pop, about 5 minutes, then add the potatoes, mushrooms, carrots and courgettes. Heat to simmering, then give the mixture a good stir. Pour in the water, season to taste and cook over very low heat for 15 minutes.
2. Meanwhile, preheat the oven to 425°F/220°C (Gas Mark 7). Grease the quiche tin. Roll out two-thirds of the pastry and fit into the tin, leaving enough pastry at the top edge to form a good seal with the lid.
3. When the vegetable mixture is cooked, remove from the heat and allow to cool slightly. Pour the filling into the tin and level the top. Roll out the remaining pastry and place over the pie, pinching the top and bottom crusts together to seal. Brush the top with beaten egg.
4. Place the pie on a baking sheet and bake for 40 minutes, or until the pie has risen and the top is golden-brown. Remove from the oven and allow to cool.
5. Pack the pie in its tin. To serve, unmould and slice when you have reached the picnic site.

PASTA SALAD

Preparation time: 8–10 minutes
Cooking time: 10 minutes
Chilling time: 2 hours

IMPERIAL (METRIC)
½ lb large pasta shells or *bows*
*1 green pepper, deseeded and thinly
    sliced*
1 egg yolk
1 tablespoonful walnut oil
1 tablespoonful wine vinegar
2 cloves garlic, crushed
¼ pint (140ml) soured cream or
    Greek yogurt
1 bunch spring onions, chopped
*Sea salt and freshly ground black
    pepper*

AMERICAN
½ lb large pasta shells or *bow-ties*
*1 green pepper, seeded and thinly
    sliced*
1 egg yolk
1 tablespoonful walnut oil
1 tablespoonful wine vinegar
2 cloves garlic, crushed
⅔ cup sour cream or *Greek yogurt*
1 bunch scallions, chopped
*Sea salt and freshly ground black
    pepper*

1. Bring a large saucepan of lightly salted water to the boil over moderate heat and add the pasta. Cook for about 8 minutes or until it is just tender. Drain thoroughly in a colander.
2. In a large bowl, combine the egg yolk, oil, vinegar and garlic. Gradually add the soured cream or yogurt, beating constantly. Toss the pasta, green pepper and spring onions in the dressing, season to taste and mix thoroughly.
3. Pack the pasta salad in an airtight container and refrigerate for at least 2 hours or until needed.

GREEN LEAF SALAD

Use a variety of whatever leaves are in season. Tear into manageable pieces and store in an airtight bag or container. Make a good, strong vinaigrette dressing to be carried separately in a small plastic bottle.

PEARS STUFFED WITH STILTON

Preparation time: minimal
Chilling time: 1 hours

IMPERIAL (METRIC)
4–6 large pears
4 oz (115g) Stilton cheese, at room
   temperature
1 oz (30g) butter, softened
Freshly ground black pepper

AMERICAN
4–6 large pears
¼ lb Stilton or other blue-veined
   cheese, at room temperature
2 tablespoonsful butter, softened
Freshly ground black pepper

1. Make sure that the pears are just ripe, but not too soft.
2. Do not peel the pears, but cut them in half, remove the stalk and core.
3. In a small bowl, combine the cheese and butter, mashing to a smooth paste and adding plenty of freshly ground pepper. Fill the pear cavities with the cheese mixture and immediately cover each half individually with cling film.
4. Refrigerate until needed, then pack carefully and snugly.

HOT BUTTERED RUM

Serves 4
Cooking time: 15 minutes

IMPERIAL (METRIC)
1 oz (30g) butter
2 tablespoonsful soft brown sugar
½ teaspoonful ground cloves
Pinch of ground cinnamon
Pinch of grated nutmeg
Pinch of allspice
¼ pint (140ml) water
Zest and juice of 1 orange
Zest and juice of 1 lemon
½ pint (285ml) dark rum

AMERICAN
2 tablespoonsful butter
2 tablespoonsful soft brown sugar
½ teaspoonful ground cloves
Pinch of ground cinnamon
Pinch of grated nutmeg
Pinch of allspice
⅔ cup water
Zest and juice of 1 orange
Zest and juice of 1 lemon
1¼ cups dark rum

1. Melt the butter in a medium-sized saucepan over low heat. Add the sugar and stir until it is dissolved. Add the cloves, cinnamon, nutmeg, allspice and water and then the orange and lemon zest. Increase the heat to moderate and bring to the boil, then simmer for 2–3 minutes. Pour in the orange and lemon juice and the rum. Return to the boil, then remove from the heat.
2. Strain the mixture through a sieve and pour into a vacuum flask.

A COLD DAY AT THE RACES

As I know nothing about racing and have rarely attended these events, I use the name of this picnic to signify any occasion like a gala sports day when the weather is chilly and you need to celebrate with a picnic meal that will warm the body and the spirit.

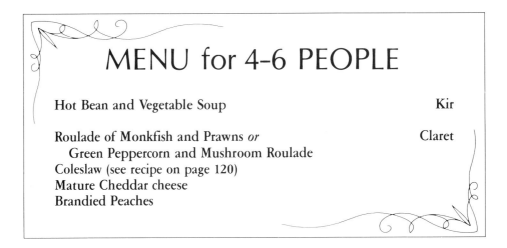

MENU for 4-6 PEOPLE

Hot Bean and Vegetable Soup   Kir

Roulade of Monkfish and Prawns *or*   Claret
    Green Peppercorn and Mushroom Roulade
Coleslaw (see recipe on page 120)
Mature Cheddar cheese
Brandied Peaches

HOT BEAN AND VEGETABLE SOUP

Soaking time:	overnight
Preparation time:	20 minutes
Cooking time:	1 hour

IMPERIAL (METRIC)	AMERICAN
½ lb (225g) potatoes	*½ lb potatoes*
2 large onions	*2 large onions*
1 head celery	*1 head celery*
2 large leeks	*2 large leeks*
1 oz (30g) butter	*2 tablespoonsful butter*
2 tablespoonsful olive oil	*2 tablespoonsful olive oil*
4 oz (115g) dried haricot beans, soaked overnight	*½ cup dried navy beans, soaked overnight*
2½ pints (1.5 litres) water	*6 cups water*
¼ pint (140ml) dry white wine or vermouth	*⅔ cup dry white wine or vermouth*
Sea salt and freshly ground black pepper	*Sea salt and freshly ground black pepper*
Generous handful of parsley, finely chopped	*Generous handful of parsley, finely chopped*

1. Peel and dice the potatoes. Slice the onions, celery and leeks thinly.
2. Heat the butter and olive oil together in a large saucepan and add the beans and vegetables. Sauté for a few minutes, then pour in the water and bring to the boil. Reduce the heat and simmer for 1 hour, until the beans are just tender. Add the white wine or vermouth and season to taste. Stir in the parsley.
3. Remove from the heat and pour into a large vacuum flask.

ROULADE OF MONKFISH AND PRAWNS

Preparation time: 15 minutes
Baking time: 30–35 minutes

IMPERIAL (METRIC)
½ lb (225g) frozen puff pastry, defrosted
1 lb (455g) monkfish, skinned and boned
1 lb unshelled Mediterranean prawns
4 oz (115g) cottage cheese
1 onion, thinly sliced
2 tablespoonsful tomato purée
Sea salt and freshly ground black pepper
1 bunch dillweed or fennel, finely chopped
1 egg, beaten
Sesame seeds to sprinkle

AMERICAN
½ lb frozen puff pastry, defrosted
1 lb monkfish, skinned and boned
1 lb unshelled jumbo shrimps
½ cup cottage cheese
1 onion, thinly sliced
2 tablespoonsful tomato paste
Sea salt and freshly ground black pepper
1 bunch fresh dill or fennel, finely chopped
1 egg, beaten
Sesame seeds to sprinkle

1. Preheat the oven to 425°F/220°C (Gas Mark 7). Grease a baking sheet.
2. Roll the pastry out into a rectangle approximately 12 × 15 inches (30 × 37.5cm).
3. Chop the monkfish coarsely and place in a large bowl. Remove the heads from the prawns and squeeze their juices over the monkfish. Shell the prawns and add to the bowl with the cottage cheese, onion and tomato purée. Season to taste and add the dillweed or fennel. Stir well.
4. Spread the fish mixture evenly over the pastry and roll up carefully and neatly like a Swiss roll. Place on the baking sheet with the seam underneath, brush with beaten egg and sprinkle with sesame seeds.
5. Bake for 30–35 minutes or until puffed up and golden-brown. Remove from the oven and set aside to cool.
6. Wrap the roulade in cling film and refrigerate until needed.

GREEN PEPPERCORN AND MUSHROOM ROULADE

Preparation time: 15 minutes
Cooking time: 5 minutes
Baking time: 30–35 minutes

IMPERIAL (METRIC)
*½ lb (225g) frozen puff pastry,
  defrosted
1 oz (30g) butter
1 lb (455g) mushrooms, sliced
2 onions, thinly sliced
4 oz (115g) cottage cheese
2 tablespoonsful green peppercorns
1 bunch parsley, finely chopped
Sea salt and freshly ground black
  pepper
1 egg, beaten
Sesame seeds*

AMERICAN
*½ lb frozen puff pastry, defrosted
2 tablespoonsful butter
1 lb mushrooms, sliced
2 onions, thinly sliced
½ cup cottage cheese
2 tablespoonsful green peppercorns
1 bunch parsley, finely chopped
Sea salt and freshly ground black
  pepper
1 egg, beaten
Sesame seeds*

1. Preheat the oven to 425°F/220°C (Gas Mark 7). Grease a baking sheet.
2. Roll out the pastry thinly to a rectangle, approximately 12 × 15 inches (30 × 27.5cm).
3. Melt the butter in a medium-sized saucepan. Add the mushrooms and onions and sauté until soft, about 5 minutes. Remove from the heat and set aside to cool.
4. Add the cheese, peppercorns and parsley to the mushroom mixture. Mix well and season to taste. Spread the mixture over the pastry and roll up carefully and neatly like a Swiss roll. Place on the baking sheet with the seam underneath and brush with beaten egg and sprinkle with sesame seeds.
5. Bake for 30–35 minutes or until puffed up and golden-brown. Remove from the oven and set aside to cool.
6. Wrap the roulade in cling film and refrigerate until needed.

BRANDIED PEACHES

Preparation time: minimal
Cooking time: 15 minutes

IMPERIAL (METRIC)	AMERICAN
1 oz (30g) butter	*2 tablespoonful butter*
¼ teaspoonful ground cloves	*¼ teaspoonful ground cloves*
¼ teaspoonful ground allspice	*¼ teaspoonful ground allspice*
2 tablespoonful soft brown sugar	*2 tablespoonful soft brown sugar*
½ pint (140ml) brandy	*⅔ cup brandy*
4–6 ripe peaches	*4–6 ripe peaches*
Whipped cream to serve	*Whipped cream to serve*

1. Melt the butter in a medium-sized saucepan over moderate heat. Add the cloves, allspice and sugar and stir well. Pour in the brandy and bring to the boil, then reduce the heat to a simmer and stir for a few minutes.
2. Cut the peaches in half, remove the stones and add to the brandy mixture. Return to the boil, then simmer for 3–4 minutes. Remove from the heat, leave the peaches to cool in the liquid, then refrigerate in a suitable container.
3. Just before packing up the picnic, whip the cream and place in a small pot.
4. Serve the brandied peaches with a dollop of whipped cream.

A BUFFET IN THE GARDEN

For every decade that comes around now, I give a large birthday party in my garden. I have been very lucky, because this particular day in July, so far, has always been fine and sunny.

People think that a buffet party for up to a hundred guests is a mammoth task. It need not be with proper planning and lots of help.

Decide on the dishes you will serve and start shopping for the ingredients four days in advance. Most of the cooking can be done two to three days beforehand. Shop the day before the party for fresh fruits and vegetables. On the morning of the party, if possible, enlist someone else to shop for the cheeses.

A good ploy is to prepare and cook many small dishes to begin the meal. Starters in the Chinese or Middle Eastern tradition always appeal.

Have a large platter of crudités (prepared immediately before the party) and a large variety of purées that guests can eat with bread, biscuits, pitta bread or the crudités.

The next course could be pâté, a terrine and a mousse — maybe even two of each. With those, I would offer a tart, pie or quiche.

If fish were on the menu, I think I would have salmon made into gravlax and, if possible, a cold spiced fish stew. For a barbecue, I might grill a whole white fish, like bass, or offer a selection of raw fish chunks for guests to skewer and cook themselves.

I would also offer plenty of salad — for example, potato, pasta, tabbouleh, a huge mixed green salad, a many-coloured bitter leaf salad, tomato and basil, cucumber and yogurt, a fruit and vegetable salad, coleslaw, and a Greek salad.

End the meal with a variety of cheeses and fresh fruit, or a large fresh fruit salad, or fruit sorbets and ice cream, or fruit tarts or fools.

Do not attempt to make each dish in a quantity sufficient to feed a hundred people. This would be absurd and make for a dull party with lots of food left over. Plan for each dish to feed a dozen people and offer a lot of variety. This way, the amounts of any particular dish are not overpowering and the flavours can be adjusted so they are just right. When cooking a large quantity of food, it is often difficult to judge the flavour properly.

Many recipes suitable for a buffet party can be found throughout this book — others I offer in this chapter.

Now a word on presentation. Try to provide plenty of chairs and tables scattered around the garden as well as the large tables on which you will arrange the food. Make it clear to the guests that they can sit, stand or roam around wherever they are happiest. Decorate the tables with fresh flowers. *Never* use disposable cutlery or plates; it looks cheap and unpleasant. Either beg, borrow or hire whatever you need. Offer litres of red and white wine on the tables and jugs of iced fruit juice. In the summer it is also agreeable to have iced tea or coffee.

MENU FOR 100 PEOPLE

Chinese or Middle Eastern-type appetizers
Crudités
Purées
Selection of bread and biscuits
Pâtés
Terrines
Mousses
Tarts, pies or quiches
Gravlax or Pickled Fish
Indonesian Spiced Fish Casserole
West Indian Casserole
A good selection of salads
Cheese and a fruit dessert

White wine, red wine,
iced fruit juice,
iced tea or coffee

TARAMASALATA

Preparation time: 20 minutes

IMPERIAL (METRIC)
1 lb (455g) smoked cod's roe
Zest and juice of 1 lemon
2 cloves garlic, crushed
½ pint (285ml) olive oil
Sea salt and freshly ground black
  pepper
4 oz (115g) cream cheese

AMERICAN
1 lb smoked cod's roe
Zest and juice of 1 lemon
2 cloves garlic, crushed
1¼ cups olive oil
Sea salt and freshly ground black
  pepper
4 oz cream cheese

1. Skin the roe and place in a blender container. Add the lemon zest, juice and garlic and blend until smooth.
2. Add the olive oil slowly, as if you were making mayonnaise. When all of the olive oil is incorporated, season to taste and add the cream cheese and blend again.
3. Refrigerate until needed. This is one of the best purées in the world.

TAPENADE

Preparation time: 10 minutes

IMPERIAL (METRIC)
1 tin anchovies, undrained
4 oz (115g) capers
6 black olives, stoned
Zest and juice of 1 lemon
3 cloves garlic, crushed
Fresh ground black pepper
Olive oil

AMERICAN
1 can anchovies, undrained
½ cup capers
6 black olives, stoned
Zest and juice of 1 lemon
3 cloves garlic, crushed
Fresh ground black pepper
Olive oil

1. Place the undrained anchovies and capers in a blender container and blend.
2. Add the olives, lemon zest and juice and garlic and blend again.
3. Add pepper to taste and enough oil to make a thick purée. Do not add salt. There should be enough in the anchovies, capers and olives.
4. Refrigerate until needed.

ANCHOVY PASTE

Preparation time: 5 minutes

IMPERIAL (METRIC)
3–4 tins anchovies
Freshly ground black pepper
Zest and juice of 1 lemon
3 cloves garlic, crushed

AMERICAN
3–4 cans anchovies
Freshly ground black pepper
Zest and juice of 1 lemon
3 cloves garlic, crushed

1. Place all the ingredients in a blender container and blend to a rough but thick purée.
2. Refrigerate until needed.

PRAWN PASTE

Preparation time: 15 minutes
Cooking time: 15 minutes

IMPERIAL (METRIC)
1½ lb (680g) unshelled cooked
    prawns
Zest and juice of 1 lemon
Sea salt and freshly ground black
    pepper
4 oz (115g) Quark

AMERICAN
1½ lb unshelled cooked shrimp
Zest and juice of 1 lemon
Sea salt and freshly ground black
    pepper
4 oz low fat cream cheese

1. Shell the prawns. Place the shells in a saucepan, cover with water, place over moderate heat and simmer for 10 minutes. Drain liquid and reserve. Discard shells.
2. Place the prawns (reserving a few for garnish) in a blender container with the liquid from the shells and the lemon zest and juice. Blend thoroughly, then season to taste and add the cheese. Mix well.
3. Refrigerate until needed, using the reserved prawns as a garnish.

HUMMOUS I

Note: This recipe will take far less time to prepare if you used tinned chickpeas. However, that would provide you with very little hummous, so I have offered an alternative using the real thing. If you choose to use tinned chickpeas, eliminate the soaking and cooking times.

Soaking time: overnight
Preparation time: 10 minutes
Cooking time: 2 hours

IMPERIAL (METRIC)
6 oz (170g) dried chickpeas, soaked
    overnight, or 2×14 oz (395g) tins
Zest and juice of 1 lemon
3 cloves garlic, crushed
¼–½ pint (140–285ml) olive oil
Sea salt and freshly ground black
    pepper
3 tablespoonsful tahini (sesame paste)
    (optional)

AMERICAN
1 scant cup dried garbanzo beans,
    soaked overnight or 28 oz canned
    chickpeas
Zest and juice of 1 lemon
3 cloves garlic, crushed
⅔–1¼ cups olive oil
Sea salt and freshly ground black
    pepper
3 tablespoonsful tahini (sesame paste)
    (optional)

1. If you are using dried chickpeas, drain, then place in a saucepan with plenty of boiling water and cook for 2 hours, or until tender. Drain.
2. Place the chickpeas in a blender container with the lemon zest and juice, garlic and olive oil. (If you are using tinned chickpeas, they will absorb barely ¼ pint (140ml). If you are using dried chickpeas, add ½ pint (285ml). Blend to a smooth purée, season to taste and add the tahini if desired. (I find the flavour of hummous so refreshing on its own that I don't want it altered by the tahini.) Mix well.
3. Refrigerate until needed.

HUMMOUS II

Soaking time:	overnight
Preparation time:	10 minutes
Cooking time:	2 hours

IMPERIAL (METRIC)
½ lb dried chick peas, soaked
* overnight*
1 large onion, roughly chopped
2 bay leaves
½ pint natural yogurt
2 tablespoonsful olive oil
3 cloves garlic, crushed
1 teaspoonful cumin seeds, crushed
Zest and juice of 1 lemon
Sea salt and freshly ground black
* pepper*

AMERICAN
1¼ cups dried garbanzo beans,
* soaked overnight*
1 large onion, roughly chopped
2 bay leaves
1¼ cups plain yogurt
2 tablespoonsful olive oil
3 cloves garlic, crushed
1 teaspoonful cumin seeds, crushed
Zest and juice of 1 lemon
Sea salt and freshly ground black
* pepper*

1. Drain the chickpeas, then place in a saucepan with plenty of boiling water and cook for 2 hours, or until tender. Drain. Discard the bay leaves.
2. Place the chickpeas and onion in a blender container. Blend to a purée. Add the remaining ingredients and blend again.
3. Refrigerate until needed.

MELITZANA (Aubergine Purée)

Preparation time:	5 minutes
Cooking time:	2 hours

IMPERIAL (METRIC)
2 large aubergines
¼ pint (140ml) olive oil
Zest and juice of 1 lemon
3 cloves garlic, crushed
Sea salt and freshly ground black
* pepper*

AMERICAN
2 large eggplants
⅔ cup olive oil
Zest and juice of 1 lemon
3 cloves garlic, crushed
Sea salt and freshly ground black
* pepper*

1. Brush the skins of the aubergines with a little of the oil. Place the aubergines in a baking dish.
2. Set the oven temperature to 275°F/140°C (Gas Mark 1). Bake the aubergines for about 2 hours, or until the flesh is soft. Remove from the oven and allow to cool.
3. Scoop out all of the aubergine flesh into a blender container. Add the remaining ingredients and blend to a smooth, creamy purée.
4. Refrigerate until needed.

CHILLI BEANS

Soaking time: overnight
Preparation time: 5 minutes
Cooking time: 1¼ hours

IMPERIAL (METRIC)
6 oz (170g) dried red kidney beans,
*   soaked overnight*
2 dried red chillies, ground
3 cloves garlic, crushed
Zest and juice of 1 lemon
¼ pint (140ml) olive oil
Sea salt and freshly ground black
*   pepper*
4 oz (115g) Quark

AMERICAN
1 scant cup dried red kidney beans,
*   soaked overnight*
2 dried red chilies, ground
3 cloves garlic, crushed
Zest and juice of 1 lemon
⅔ cup olive oil
Sea salt and freshly ground black
*   pepper*
4 oz low fat cream cheese

1. Drain the kidney beans. Place in a medium-sized saucepan with plenty of water and bring to the boil. Boil fiercely for 10 minutes, then drain. Cover with fresh water, add the chillies and simmer for 1 hour, or until the beans are tender. Remove from the heat and drain.
2. Transfer the beans to a blender container and add the garlic, lemon, zest and juice and seasoning. Blend, adding the oil a little at a time, until the beans are puréed.
3. Add the cheese and mix thoroughly.
4. Refrigerate until needed.

JAJIKI

Preparation time: 10 minutes
Standing time: 1 hour

IMPERIAL (METRIC)
2 large cucumbers
Sea salt
1 pint (570ml) natural yogurt or half
*   each of yogurt and smetana*
Handful of mint, finely chopped
Freshly ground black pepper

AMERICAN
4 cucumbers
Sea salt
2½ cups plain yogurt or half each of
*   yogurt and low-fat sour cream*
Handful of mint, finely chopped
Freshly ground black pepper

1. Chop the cucumbers and place in a colander. Sprinkle with salt and set aside for 1 hour.
2. Rinse the cucumbers under the cold tap and dry with tea towels. Place in a large bowl and add the yogurt (or yogurt and smetana for a richer mixture). Stir in the mint and season with pepper.
3. Refrigerate until needed. This is a highly refreshing summer purée.

GRAVLAX

A simple recipe for gravlax is best. This one comes from the Norwegian fish markets, where the wild salmon comes in fresh every day. Other gravlax recipes pickle the fish so that it is no longer raw.

    Preparation time: 1 hour (30 minutes each before and after marinating)
    Standing time: 24 hours

IMPERIAL (METRIC)	AMERICAN
1 whole fresh farmed or *wild salmon*	*1 whole fresh farmed* or *wild salmon*
Coarse sea salt	*Coarse sea salt*
Generous bunch of fresh chopped dillweed	*Generous bunch of fresh chopped dill*

1. Fillet the salmon: remove the head and discard. Carefully separate both sides of the flesh from the backbone, leaving the skin intact. (Or get your fishmonger to do this, but sometimes they are inept and throw away much of the salmon flesh with the backbone; this is an expensive waste.)
2. Scatter both sides of the filleted salmon with sea salt and plenty of chopped dillweed. (Be generous with the dillweed, ensuring that the green herb covers all the orange flesh.)
3. Roll up each fillet tightly, cover and place in the refrigerator for 24 hours.
4. To serve, wipe the fillets and scrape away the salt and dillweed, then slice very thinly like smoked salmon.

PICKLED SALMON

Pickled salmon is another treat altogether.

    Preparation time: 1 hour (30 minutes each before and after marinating)
    Marinating time: 3 days

IMPERIAL (METRIC)	AMERICAN
1 whole fresh farmed or *wild salmon, filleted as in Gravlax recipe, (see above)*	*1 whole fresh farmed* or *wild salmon, filleted as in Gravlax recipe, (see above)*
1 tablespoonful castor sugar	*1 tablespoonful superfine sugar*
1 tablespoonful sea salt	*1 tablespoonful sea salt*
½ tablespoonful black peppercorns	*½ tablespoonful black peppercorns*
½ tablespoonful white peppercorns	*½ tablespoonful white peppercorns*
1 tablespoonful mustard powder	*1 tablespoonful mustard powder*
Generous handful of fresh chopped dillweed	*Generous handful of fresh chopped dill*
Juice of 1 lemon	*Juice of 1 lemon*
3 fl oz brandy	*3 fl oz brandy*

1. Place one of the salmon fillets skin-side down in a non-metal dish.
2. Combine the sugar, salt, peppercorns, mustard powder and dillweed and rub into the

salmon flesh. Place the other salmon fillet on top, skin-side up and pour over the lemon juice and brandy. Cover with cling film, then with a board or heavy plate and weight down with a brick or similar heavy weight.

3. Marinate in the refrigerator for 3 days, turning the salmon and basting twice a day with the marinade to prevent the fish from drying out.
4. To serve, scrape away the dillweed and seasonings, then slice very thinly like smoked salmon.

INDONESIAN SPICED FISH CASSEROLE

Preparation time: 10 minutes
Cooking time: 40 minutes

IMPERIAL (METRIC)	AMERICAN
3 lb (1.5 kg) firm white fish, boned and skinned	3 lb firm white fish, boned and skinned
Seasoned flour to coat	Seasoned flour to coat
3 tablespoonsful olive oil	3 tablespoonsful olive oil
1 teaspoonful each: mustard seeds, ground turmeric, fenugreek and ground cumin	1 teaspoonful each: mustard seeds, ground turmeric, fenugreek and ground cumin
2 oz (55g) fresh root ginger, peeled and thinly sliced	1 3-inch piece fresh ginger root, pared and thinly sliced
3 cloves garlic, thinly sliced	3 cloves garlic, thinly sliced
2 onions, thinly sliced	2 onions, thinly sliced
2 green peppers, deseeded and sliced	2 green peppers, seeded and sliced
2½ pints (1.4 litres) water	6 cups water
2 lb (900g) new potatoes, sliced	2 lb new potatoes, sliced
1 lb (455g) fresh mushrooms, wiped clean and sliced	1 lb fresh mushrooms, wiped clean and sliced
¼ oz (7g) creamed coconut, grated	2 tablespoonsful grated creamed coconut

1. Cut the fish into chunks and roll in the seasoned flour. Set aside.
2. Heat the oil in a large casserole. Add the mustard seeds, turmeric, fenugreek, cumin, ginger, garlic, onions and peppers. Sauté for a few minutes, then add the coated fish. Turn around in the spices for a moment, then add the water and bring to the boil. Add the potatoes and mushrooms and simmer for 30 minutes.
3. Add the creamed coconut and stir until the sauce thickens. Remove from the heat and leave to cool.
4. Refrigerate until needed. Serve cold with rice.

Note: If some of your guests are vegetarians, you can omit the fish from the Indonesian Spiced Fish Casserole and add chickpeas, pulses and other vegetables. An alternative recipe for a West Indian vegetable casserole follows. It can be eaten hot, warm, or cold and makes a marvellous centrepiece.

WEST INDIAN CASSEROLE

Soaking time: overnight
Cooking time: 2½ hours

IMPERIAL (METRIC)	AMERICAN
6 oz (170g) chickpeas, soaked overnight	¾ cup garbanzo beans, soaked overnight
6 oz (170g) dried black beans, soaked overnight	¾ cup dried black beans, soaked overnight
3 tablespoonsful corn oil	3 tablespoonsful corn oil
2 oz (55g) fresh root ginger, peeled and grated	½ cup grated fresh ginger root
5 cloves garlic, crushed	5 cloves garlic, crushed
1 teaspoonful cumin seeds	1 teaspoonful cumin seeds
1 teaspoonful mustard seeds	1 teaspoonful mustard seeds
1 teaspoonful whole cloves	1 teaspoonful whole cloves
1 teaspoonful ground turmeric	1 teaspoonful ground turmeric
2 cinnamon sticks	2 cinnamon sticks
3 onions, chopped coarsely	3 onions, chopped coarsely
2 lb (900g) potatoes, peeled and chopped	2 lb potatoes, peeled and chopped
½ lb (225g) French beans, trimmed and chopped	½ lb beans, trimmed and chopped
1 cabbage, chopped	1 cabbage, chopped
1 cauliflower, separated into florets	1 cauliflower, separated into florets
4 tablespoonsful tomato purée	4 tablespoonsful tomato paste
1 teaspoonful sea salt	1 teaspoonful sea salt
3 oz (85g) creamed coconut, grated	¾ cup grated creamed coconut

1. Drain the chickpeas and place in a large saucepan with plenty of fresh water. Bring to the boil over moderate heat, then simmer for 2 hours (or cook in a pressure cooker for 20 minutes). Remove from the heat and set aside, without draining.

2. Meanwhile, drain the black beans and place in another large saucepan with plenty of fresh water. Bring to the boil over a high heat and boil fiercely for 10 minutes. Remove from the heat, drain, discard the water and fill the saucepan with fresh water. Return the beans to the saucepan and simmer over moderate heat for 1 hour or until tender. Remove from the heat and set aside, without draining.

3. Heat the corn oil in a flameproof casserole over low heat. Add the ginger, garlic, cumin, mustard seeds, cloves, turmeric and cinnamon sticks. Sauté for a few minutes until the mustard seeds pop, then add the onions, potatoes, cabbage and the cooking water from the chickpeas and black beans. Bring to the boil over moderate heat, then simmer for 15 minutes. Add the cauliflower, tomato purée and salt. Simmer for 5 minutes, then add the chickpeas and black beans. Stir and simmer for a further 3 minutes. Finally, stir in the creamed coconut and simmer for 2 minutes. Remove from the heat and allow to cool.

Note: This casserole is best made the day before and reheated on the day of the buffet. Or it can be served cold with a pilaf or rice salad.

MOVABLE FEASTS

Airline Travel

Although airlines are slowly improving the quality of their food and you can now order vegetarian meals in advance, it is really much nicer to take your own picnic.

What you eat or drink on an aeroplane can easily increase the discomfort of the journey. Flying is an unnatural form of travel for the human body, and it responds to the stress.

The pressure of the aircraft causes the gases in our system to expand; do not add to them by consuming fizzy drinks, either soft drinks or champagne.

The dehydration of the filtered air we breathe puts our kidneys (which regulate the balance of water in the blood) under strain. It is best to drink a lot of water; half a pint (one quarter of a litre) every hour or so is about right. Avoid alcohol. It makes the liver work harder and increases dehydration. Smoking is bad for the system also, as it increases the amount of carbon monoxide in the body.

To offset this, plan ahead and take food with you that is low in protein and rather bland (rich foods place strain on the digestion) that will refresh the body rather than oppress it. The food should be light and delicious, washed down with still mineral water or herb tea. If you carry several teabags of herb tea, the cabin crew will be glad to provide you with hot water.

MENU FOR 2 PEOPLE

Chilled Parsnip and Orange Soup
Prawn Pilaf with lettuce leaves
 or Fresh Pea and Fungi Pilaf with lettuce leaves
Petit Suisse cheese with grapes and cherries

PARSNIP AND ORANGE SOUP

Preparation time: minimal
Cooking time: 15 minutes
Chilling time: 2 hour

IMPERIAL (METRIC)
1 lb (455g) parsnips, trimmed and chopped
1 pint (570ml) vegetable stock
Zest and juice of 4 oranges
Sea salt and freshly ground black pepper

AMERICAN
1 lb parsnips, trimmed and chopped
2½ cups vegetable stock
Zest and juice of 4 oranges
Sea salt and freshly ground black pepper

1. Place the parsnips in a medium-sized saucepan with the vegetable stock and bring to the boil. Simmer until tender, about 8 minutes. Add the orange zest, season to taste and simmer for a further 2 minutes.
2. Place the contents of the saucepan in a blender container and blend until smooth. Add the orange juice.
3. Refrigerate until needed, then pour into a vacuum flask.

PRAWN PILAF

Preparation time: 10 minutes
Cooking time: 30 minutes

IMPERIAL (METRIC)
1 lb (455g) unshelled cooked prawns
1 pint (570ml) water
4 oz (115g) millet
½ lb (225g) frozen broad beans
1 red pepper, deseeded and finely sliced
1 green pepper, deseeded and finely sliced
1 bunch spring onions, finely chopped
Zest and juice of 1 lemon
2 tablespoonsful olive oil
Sea salt and freshly ground black pepper
Lettuce leaves to serve

AMERICAN
1 lb unshelled cooked shrimps
2½ cups water
4 oz millet
½ lb frozen fava or lima beans
1 red pepper, seeded and finely sliced
1 green pepper, seeded and finely sliced
1 bunch scallions, finely chopped
⅔ cup millet
Zest and juice of 1 lemon
2 tablespoonsful olive oil
Sea salt and freshly ground black pepper
Lettuce leaves to serve

1. Shell the prawns. Place the shells in a saucepan, add the water and boil for 10 minutes. Drain the shells, reserving the cooking liquid and discarding the shells.
2. Cook the millet over low heat in the prawn liquid for 15 minutes. Remove from the heat and allow to stand until cool, when all the liquid should be absorbed.
3. Meanwhile, cook the beans until tender in a small amount of salted water.
4. Add the prawns, beans, red and green peppers, and spring onions to the millet and mix thoroughly.

5. Mix together in a cup the lemon zest and juice and olive oil. Pour over the pilaf and season to taste.
6. Place in a container with a tightly fitting lid. To eat, scoop up the pilaf with the lettuce leaves, which should be a crisp variety.

FRESH PEA AND FUNGI PILAF

Soaking time: overnight
Preparation time: 10 minutes
Cooking time: 25 minutes

IMPERIAL (METRIC)
1 lb (455g) fresh peas
4 oz (115g) dried fungi, soaked
  overnight
4 oz (115g) millet
2 cloves garlic, crushed
1½ pints (850ml) vegetable stock
1 bunch spring onions, finely
  chopped
Zest and juice of 1 lemon
2 tablespoonsful olive oil
Sea salt and freshly ground black
  pepper
Lettuce leaves to serve

AMERICAN
1 lb fresh peas
4 oz dried fungi, soaked overnight
4 oz millet
2 cloves garlic crushed
1 quart vegetable stock
1 bunch scallions, finely chopped
Zest and juice of 1 lemon
2 tablespoonsful olive oil
Sea salt and freshly ground black
  pepper
Lettuce leaves to serve

1. Chop up the dried fungi. Pod the peas and boil them together in a small amount of water for 7 minutes. Drain, reserving any liquid.
2. Cook the millet with the garlic using the liquid from the peas and fungi. Add the vegetable stock and simmer for 15 minutes.
3. Mix the fungi, peas and spring onions with the millet.
4. Mix together in a cup the lemon zest, juice, olive oil and seasoning. Pour over the pilaf.
5. Place in a container with a tightly fitting lid. To eat, scoop up the pilaf with the lettuce leaves, which should be a crisp variety.

End the meal with Petit Suisse cheese, grapes and cherries, a delicious and trouble-free dessert.

Ferry Crossings

I have tried the food on many ferries and found it overpriced and not at all good in terms of quality; certainly not to my taste. I prefer to take my own picnic, at least until the catering improves sufficiently.

Sandwiches made from fresh bread with any of the fillings on pages 71–80 are the most practical.

If you don't have time to prepare sandwich fillings before starting out, there are excellent vegetarian pâtés on the market which can be used in sandwiches with crisp lettuce, tomato and cucumber. The simplest and most obvious combinations often make the nicest picnics.

But if you have to cook, any of the pies and tarts in this book, plus a salad, make a good, quick picnic, as do many other suggestions in these pages.

On the Road in France

Some of the best picnics in my lifetime have been enjoyed while motoring through France, the food chosen from market stalls or corner shops. (It is difficult, I admit, to ignore the charcuterie, but the reasons for omitting meat from one's diet apply as much to French meat as they do to British meat. If you remind yourself of these points and consider the odds and ends that go into sausage making, the products of the charcuterie become a great deal less palatable.)

In my car is a picnic hamper containing sea salt, a pepper mill, coffee grinder, a bowl for salad, a Calor gas ring, a small saucepan, kitchen scissors and sharp knives, a can opener, a corkscrew, a kitchen roll, cutlery, glasses and plates wrapped in tea towels. I also have a rug to sit on and a few cushions for comfort.

Outside of the car, the whole of France is to be enjoyed. The food is a movable feast, since I take the trouble to find regional delicacies.

The vegetables for salad always seem to be in peak condition — plump, ripe tomatoes, crisp lettuce, aromatic basil and firm asparagus. The mixture of salad leaves called *mesclun* has a superb fragrance and bite. Some vegetables, which we think of as always having to be cooked, can, when young, be eaten raw: globe artichokes, trimmed and cut into quarters, dipped in lemon juice and oil; courgettes sliced into sticks; young broad beans and peas, delicious eaten straight from the pod. French pickled vegetables are of high quality. Young sweetcorn, fungi and jars of mixed vegetables are all good to add to a salad.

French cheeses are legion; when travelling, opt for the local ones. Don't be afraid of trying cheeses that are new to you. Fromage frais can be bought in different percentages of fat content to be eaten and enjoyed like yogurt, or used as a basis for chopped fresh fruit.

The north and Atlantic coasts of France are well known for their fish and shellfish. Shrimps and prawns make an excellent meal and you can buy dressed crab, but most of the other marine delights will need to be cooked over a fire.

The skills of French pastry chefs are too good to be missed, such as: *Mirlitons* — almond and cream tartlets; pear and almond tarts, latticed apple and plum tarts; *Le Poirat* — walnut pear tart; *Clafoutis Limousin* — cherry flans; *pain au noix* — walnut bread; *Galettes Flamandes* — hazelnut and candied orange tartlets; *flan aux marrons* — chestnut custard tart; and many other sweet endings. For my part, I save at the charcuterie and spend at the pâtisserie.

3

SOUPS
– HOT AND COLD

Soups are a good thing to take on a picnic, for often people get thirsty and soup is a refreshing and sustaining dish. Invest in a large wide-necked vacuum flask to transport the soup and do not be frightened of being adventurous and adding a little wine or brandy — all soups will benefit from the addition.

CHILLED AVOCADO AND LEMON SOUP

Serves 6–8
Preparation time: 10 minutes
Chilling time: 2 hours

IMPERIAL (METRIC)
3 small ripe avocados (or 2 large)
Zest and juice of 2 lemons
Sea salt to taste
*½ teaspoonful freshly ground white
    pepper*
*3 pints (1.7 litres) soya milk
    (unsweetened)*
*¼ pint (140ml) soured cream or
    fromage frais*

AMERICAN
3 small ripe avocados (or 2 large)
Zest and juice of 2 lemons
Sea salt to taste
*½ teaspoonful freshly ground white
    pepper*
2 quarts soy milk (unsweetened)
⅔ cup sour cream or fromage frais

1. Peel and stone the avocados and place the flesh in a blender container. Add the zest and juice of 1 lemon, salt, pepper and soya milk and blend to a purée. Pour into a large bowl and chill in the refrigerator for 2 hours.
2. In a small bowl, mix the soured cream or fromage frais with the zest and juice of the remaining lemon. Chill in the refrigerator until needed.
3. Serve the soup chilled, passing the soured cream mixture separately for guests to help themselves.

AVOCADO AND GREEN PEPPER SOUP

Serves 6
Preparation and cooking time: 20 minutes

IMPERIAL (METRIC)
2 oz (55g) butter
*3 green peppers, cored, deseeded and
    chopped*
2 pints (1.1 litres) vegetable stock
*Sea salt and freshly ground white
    pepper*
3 small ripe avocados (or 2 large)
Chopped mint to garnish

AMERICAN
4 tablespoonsful butter
*3 green peppers, cored, seeded and
    chopped*
5 cups vegetable stock
*Sea salt and freshly ground white
    pepper*
3 small ripe avocados (or 2 large)
Chopped mint to garnish

1. Melt the butter in a medium-sized saucepan and sauté the peppers gently for 5 minutes.
2. Add the stock and salt and pepper to taste and simmer for 10 minutes.
3. Meanwhile, peel and stone the avocados and place the avocado flesh in a blender jar.
4. Add the contents of the saucepan to the blender and purée.
5. Place the avocado and pepper purée into the rinsed-out saucepan and reheat gently; the avocado must not be allowed to boil.
6. Serve hot, garnished with chopped mint.

Opposite: Danish Apple Soup (page 63).

GARLIC SOUP

Serves 4-6
Preparation time: 15 minutes
Cooking time: 1¼ hours

IMPERIAL (METRIC)
3 heads garlic
3 tablespoonsful olive oil
2 pints (1.1 litres) boiling water
Sea salt and freshly ground black
   pepper
2 egg yolks
Chopped parsley and croûtons to
   garnish (optional)

AMERICAN
3 heads garlic
3 tablespoonsful olive oil
5 cups boiling water
Sea salt and freshly ground black
   pepper
2 egg yolks
Chopped parsley and croûtons to
   garnish (optional)

1. Break the heads of garlic into separate cloves and place in a bowl. Pour boiling water over them and leave to soak for 1 minute, then pour off the water and peel the garlic. (The skins will slip off easily.)
2. Pat the garlic dry with absorbent kitchen paper. Heat the oil in a medium-sized saucepan and sauté the garlic for 2–3 minutes. Add the boiling water and salt and pepper to taste. Reduce the heat and simmer for 1 hour. Remove from the heat and set aside to cool.
3. Pour the garlic mixture into a blender container and purée.
4. Whisk the egg yolks in a bowl. Reheat the soup gently in the rinsed-out saucepan. Pour some of the soup over the eggs and stir well. Pour the egg mixture into the saucepan and heat through gently, but do not allow it to boil, or the eggs will curdle.
5. Serve hot, garnished with chopped parsley and croûtons if desired.

Previous pages: A civilized feast from the Mountain Climb menu (pages 32 to 37).
Opposite: Pizza (page 96) and Croûtes (page 95) with Fish Fillings (pages 71 to 75).

JELLIED BEETROOT AND GINGER SOUP

Serves 4–6

Preparation time:	15 minutes
Baking time:	2½–3 hours
Chilling time:	2 hours

IMPERIAL (METRIC)	AMERICAN
1 lb (455g) raw beetroot	*1 lb raw beets*
½ white cabbage, thinly sliced	*½ white cabbage, thinly sliced*
6 cloves garlic, sliced	*6 cloves garlic, sliced*
2 oz (55g) root ginger, grated	*½ cup grated ginger root*
Sea salt and freshly ground black pepper	*Sea salt and freshly ground black pepper*
Large handful of carragheen or *2 teaspoonsful vegetarian gel powder*	*Large handful of carragheen* or *2 teaspoonsful vegetarian gel powder*
Soured cream to serve	*Sour cream to serve*

1. Preheat the oven to 350°F/180°C (Gas Mark 4).
2. Peel and slice the beetroot and place in a large ovenproof casserole, interleaved with the cabbage, garlic and ginger. Sprinkle with salt and pepper, add the carragheen and cover with enough boiling water to cover the vegetables by 2 inches (5cm).
3. Cover the casserole and bake in the oven for 2½–3 hours. (If you are using vegetarian gel powder, add to the stock at the end of the baking time and simmer for 2 minutes.)
4. Remove the casserole from the oven and strain all the liquid into a large bowl or soup tureen. (The liquid should be clear and red with a pungent and delicious flavour.) Discard the vegetables, as all their goodness has gone into the stock. Chill for at least 2 hours.
5. Serve the jellied soup with soured cream.

SPICED PUMPKIN SOUP

Serves 4–6

Preparation time:	10 minutes
Cooking time:	15 minutes, plus reheating

IMPERIAL (METRIC)	AMERICAN
2 lb (900g) pumpkin flesh or *½ large pumpkin*	*2 lb pumpkin flesh* or *½ large pumpkin*
3 oz (85g) butter	*6 tablespoonsful butter*
Sea salt and freshly ground black pepper	*Sea salt and freshly ground black pepper*
½ oz (15g) root ginger, grated	*2 tablespoonsful grated ginger root*
1 dried red chilli, broken up	*1 dried red chili pepper, broken up*
1 pint (570ml) boiling water	*2½ cups boiling water*
1 teaspoonful tamarind, dissolved in a little boiling water	*1 teaspoonful tamarind, dissolved in a little boiling water*
2 pints (1.1 litres) vegetable stock	*5 cups vegetable stock*

1. Scoop out all the pumpkin flesh and discard the seeds. Dice the flesh.
2. Melt the butter in a large saucepan over moderate heat. Add the pumpkin, salt, pepper, ginger and chilli and sauté gently for about 5 minutes, until the butter is absorbed and the pumpkin is softened.
3. Add the boiling water and tamarind and bring to the boil. Reduce the heat and simmer for 10 minutes. Remove from the heat and add the vegetable stock. Allow to cool.
4. Place the pumpkin mixture in a blender container and purée. This soup should be fairly thin, very smooth and golden in colour.
5. Reheat gently before serving.

SPICY TOMATO AND RED PEPPER SOUP

Serves 4-6
Preparation time: 10 minutes
Cooking time: 20 minutes, plus reheating

IMPERIAL (METRIC)	AMERICAN
2 tablespoonsful olive oil	*2 tablespoonsful olive oil*
2 lb (900g) tomatoes	*2 lb tomatoes*
2 red peppers, deseeded and sliced	*2 red peppers, seeded and sliced*
2 cloves garlic, crushed	*2 cloves garlic, crushed*
2 dried red chillies, crushed	*2 dried red chili peppers, crushed*
Sea salt and freshly ground black pepper	*Sea salt and freshly ground black pepper*
½ pint (285ml) vegetable stock	*1¼ cups vegetable stock*
3 fl oz brandy	*3 fl oz brandy*

1. Heat the oil in a large saucepan and add the tomatoes, red peppers and chillies. Add a little salt and pepper and sauté for 10 minutes. Add the stock and simmer for a further 10 minutes. Remove from the heat.
2. Place the mixture in a blender container and purée, then sieve, discarding the tomato pips and skin.
3. Pour back into the rinsed-out saucepan, place over moderate heat and bringly slowly back to boiling point. Serve immediately.

LEEK AND SAGE DERBY SOUP

Serves 6
Preparation time: 10 minutes
Cooking time: 15 minutes

IMPERIAL (METRIC)	AMERICAN
1½ lb (680g) leeks	*1½ lb leeks*
1 oz (30g) butter	*2 tablespoonsful butter*
2 oz (55g) Sage Derby cheese, grated	*½ cup grated Sage Derby cheese or Vermont sage cheese*
1 pint (570ml) skimmed milk	*2½ cups skim milk*
Sea salt and freshly ground black pepper	*Sea salt and freshly ground black pepper*

1. Trim, clean and chop the leeks.
2. Melt the butter in a medium-sized saucepan over low heat and sauté the leeks until soft, about 8 minutes. Add the remaining ingredients, mix well and heat through gently.

WHITE FISH SOUP

Serves 6–8
Preparation time: 20 minutes
Cooking time: 15 minutes

IMPERIAL (METRIC)
2 lb (900g) white fish, plus heads and
*   bones*
Sea salt and freshly ground black
*   pepper*
1 bay leaf
Zest of 1 lemon
1 pint (570ml) water
1 pint (570ml) skimmed milk

AMERICAN
2 lb white fish, plus heads and bones
Sea salt and freshly ground black
*   pepper*
1 bay leaf
Zest of 1 lemon
2½ cups water
2½ cups skim milk

1. Place the fish and fish trimmings, seasoning, bay leaf and lemon zest in a large saucepan with the measured water. Bring to the boil over moderate heat, reduce the heat and simmer for 10 minutes.
2. Remove from the heat and leave to cool.
3. Strain the fish from the stock and reserve the stock. Discard the fish heads, skin and bones and cut the fish fillets into small chunks.
4. Place the fish stock in the rinsed out saucepan, add the fish and skimmed milk. Mix well and check the seasoning. Reheat gently.

SHELLFISH SOUP

Serves 4–6
Preparation time: 10 minutes
Cooking time: 20 minutes

IMPERIAL (METRIC)
½ lb (225g) unshelled prawns
½ lb (225g) unshelled fresh shrimps
1 pint (570ml) water
4 scallops
¼ pint (140ml) dry sherry
½ pint (285ml) skimmed milk
2 tablespoonsful smetana
Sea salt and freshly ground black
  pepper

AMERICAN
½ lb unshelled jumbo shrimps
½ lb unshelled small shrimps
2½ cups water
4 sea scallops
⅔ cup dry sherry
1¼ cups skim milk
2 tablespoonsful low-fat sour cream
Sea salt and freshly ground black
  pepper

1. Place the prawns and shrimps together with the measured water in a blender container. Blend at high speed for a few minutes.
2. Pour the contents of the blender container into a medium-sized saucepan, place over moderate heat and bring to the boil. Reduce the heat and simmer for 10 minutes. Remove from the heat and set aside to cool. Blend again, then pour the contents through a sieve, discard the broken shells and reserve the purée.
3. Chop the scallops coarsely and poach them in the rinsed-out saucepan with the sherry. Add the prawn purée, then the milk. Stir in the smetana and season to taste. Place the saucepan over moderate heat and gently bring back to boiling point.

GARDEN PEA SOUP

Serves 4–6
Preparation time: 15 minutes
Cooking time: 10 minutes, plus reheating

IMPERIAL (METRIC)
2 lb (900g) fresh garden peas
1 cos lettuce
1 oz (30g) butter
2 pints (1.1 litre) skimmed milk
2 tablespoonsful smetana
Sea salt and freshly ground black
  pepper
Handful of finely chopped parsley

AMERICAN
2 lb fresh garden peas
1 romaine lettuce
2 tablespoonsful butter
5 cups skim milk
2 tablespoonsful low-fat sour cream
Sea salt and freshly ground black
  pepper
Handful of finely chopped parsley

1. Pod the peas, reserving a few pods.
2. Tear the lettuce leaves into manageable pieces.
3. Melt the butter in a medium-sized saucepan over low heat. Add the lettuce, peas and reserved pea pods. Cook gently for about 10 minutes. Remove from the heat and allow to cool.
4. Place the lettuce and pea mixture into a blender container and blend to a smooth purée.

5. Pour the purée into a rinsed-out saucepan and reheat gently.
6. Just before serving, stir in the chopped parsley, which will give the soup a beguiling speckly green colour.

MUSHROOM SOUP

Serves 4–6
Preparation time: minimal
Cooking time: 15 minutes

IMPERIAL (METRIC)	AMERICAN
1 oz (30g) butter	*2 tablespoonsful butter*
1 lb (455g) mushrooms, sliced	*1 lb mushrooms, sliced*
Sea salt and freshly ground black pepper	*Sea salt and freshly ground black pepper*
1½ pints (850ml) skimmed milk	*1 quart skim milk*

1. Melt the butter in a medium-sized saucepan over low heat. Add the mushrooms and sauté for 10 minutes. Remove from the heat.
2. Season to taste, then allow to cool.
3. Pour the milk and the sautéed mushrooms into a blender container. Blend to a purée.
4. Pour the purée into the rinsed-out saucepan and reheat slowly.

DANISH APPLE SOUP

Serves 8–10
Preparation time: 10 minutes
Cooking time: 35 minutes

IMPERIAL (METRIC)	AMERICAN
1½ lb (680g) Bramley apples	*1½ lb cooking apples*
2 oz (55g) butter	*4 tablespoonsful butter*
4 pints (2.3 litres) vegetable stock	*2½ quarts vegetable stock*
Zest and juice of 1 lemon	*Zest and juice of 1 lemon*
¼ pint (140ml) dry white wine	*⅔ cup dry white wine*
2 oz (55g) Blue Castello or other good blue-veined cheese	*2 oz Danish Blue cheese or other good blue-veined cheese*
Sea salt and freshly ground white pepper	*Sea salt and freshly ground white pepper*

1. Peel and core the apples and slice them thinly into a bowl.
2. Melt the butter in a large saucepan and add the apples. Sauté for 1–2 minutes. Add the stock, lemon zest and juice and white wine and bring to the boil. Reduce the heat and simmer for 20 minutes.
3. Add the cheese and salt and pepper to taste and simmer for a further 10 minutes.

SYRIAN CUCUMBER SOUP

Serves 4–6
Preparation time: 10 minutes
Chilling time: at least 8 hours

IMPERIAL (METRIC)
2 cucumbers
½ pint (285ml) single cream
½ pint (285ml) natural yogurt
4 cloves garlic, crushed
*Generous handful of mint, finely
   chopped*
2 tablespoonsful tarragon vinegar
*Sea salt and freshly ground black
   pepper*

AMERICAN
4 cucumbers
1¼ cups light cream
1¼ cups plain yogurt
4 cloves garlic, crushed
*Generous handful of mint, finely
   chopped*
2 tablespoonsful tarragon vinegar
*Sea salt and freshly ground black
   pepper*

1. Grate the cucumbers into a large bowl, then stir in the remaining ingredients. Mix thoroughly.
2. Chill in the refrigerator for at least 8 hours to allow the flavours to intermingle.

WATERCRESS SOUP

Serves 4–6
Preparation time: 10 minutes
Cooking time: 30 minutes
Chilling time: 2 hours

IMPERIAL (METRIC)
1 oz (30g) butter
1 oz (30g) flour
1 pint (570ml) warm vegetable stock
2 bunches watercress
½ pint (285ml) single cream
*Sea salt and freshly ground black
   pepper*

AMERICAN
2 tablespoonsful butter
¼ cup flour
2½ cups warm vegetable stock
2 bunches watercress
1¼ cups light cream
*Sea salt and freshly ground black
   pepper*

1. Melt the butter in a medium-sized saucepan over low heat. Add the flour and cook for 2 minutes, stirring gently. Slowly add the stock, stirring well until it is incorporated and the mixture is the consistency of cream. Remove from the heat.
2. Wash the watercress, chop finely and add to the saucepan. Return to the heat and cook slowly, stirring occasionally, for about 20 minutes. Remove from the heat and allow to cool.
3. Place the contents of the saucepan into a blender container and purée. Stir in the cream, season to taste, cover and chill in the refrigerator for at least 2 hours.

TOMATO AND BASIL SOUP

Serves 6
Cooking time: 15 minutes
Chilling time: 2 hours

IMPERIAL (METRIC)
2 lb (900g) tomatoes, chopped
2 cloves garlic, crushed
Handful of basil, chopped
1 pint (570ml) vegetable stock
¼ pint (140ml) dry sherry
Sea salt and freshly ground black
  pepper

AMERICAN
2 lb tomatoes, chopped
2 cloves garlic, crushed
Handful of basil, chopped
2½ cups vegetable stock
⅔ cup dry sherry
Sea salt and freshly ground black
  pepper

1. Place all the ingredients into a medium-sized saucepan over moderate heat and bring to the boil. Reduce the heat and simmer for 10 minutes. Remove from the heat and allow to cool.
2. Place the contents of the saucepan into a blender container and purée. Sieve into a bowl, cover and chill in the refrigerator for at least 2 hours.

SORREL AND CUCUMBER SOUP

Serves 4
Preparation time: 5 minutes
Cooking time: 15 minutes
Chilling time: 2 hours

IMPERIAL (METRIC)
½ lb (225g) sorrel leaves
1 large cucumber
1 pint (570ml) vegetable stock
Sea salt and freshly ground black
  pepper
3 tablespoonsful smetana

AMERICAN
½ lb sorrel leaves
2 large cucumbers
2½ cups vegetable stock
Sea salt and freshly ground black
  pepper
3 tablespoonsful low fat sour cream

1. Tear the sorrel leaves into small bits.
2. Cut the cucumber lengthways and remove the large seeds. Chop coarsely.
3. Place the sorrel, cucumber and stock into a medium-sized saucepan and season to taste. Place over moderate heat and bring to the boil. Reduce the heat and simmer for 10 minutes. Remove from the heat and allow to cool.
4. Place the contents of the saucepan into a blender container and purée. Pour into a container, stir in the smetana and chill in the refrigerator for at least 2 hours.

SIMPLE BORSCHT

Serves 6–8

Preparation time:	10 minutes
Cooking time:	1–1½ hours
Chilling time:	2 hours

IMPERIAL (METRIC)
*1½ lb (680g) raw beetroot, peeled
   and chopped
1 pint (570ml) tomato juice
1 pint (570ml) vegetable stock
Sea salt and freshly ground black
   pepper
3 tablespoonsful smetana*

AMERICAN
*1½ lb raw beets, pared and chopped
2½ cups tomato juice
2½ cups vegetable stock
Sea salt and freshly ground black
   pepper
3 tablespoonsful low fat sour cream*

1. Place the beetroot into a large saucepan, add the tomato juice and stock bring to the boil over moderate heat. Reduce the heat and simmer for 1 hour, or until the beetroot is tender. Remove from the heat, season to taste and allow to cool.
2. Place the contents of the saucepan into a blender container and blend thoroughly until smooth. Sieve into a large bowl, stir in the smetana and chill in the refrigerator for at least 2 hours.

CHERVIL SOUP

Serves 4

Preparation time:	10 minutes
Cooking time:	15 minutes
Chilling time:	2 hours

IMPERIAL (METRIC)
*Large bunch of fresh chervil
1½ pints (850ml) vegetable stock
Sea salt and freshly ground black
   pepper
2 tablespoonsful smetana*

AMERICAN
*Large bunch of fresh chervil
1 quart vegetable stock
Sea salt and freshly ground black
   pepper
2 tablespoonsful low fat sour cream*

1. Chop the chervil coarsely. Place in a medium-sized saucepan with the stock and simmer over moderate heat for 10 minutes. Remove from the heat, season to taste and allow to cool.
2. Place the contents of the saucepan into a blender container and purée. Pour into a container, stir in the smetana and chill in the refrigerator for at least 2 hours.

Note: This is a delicious and delicate soup.

CARROT SOUP

Serves 6

Preparation time: 10 minutes
Cooking time: 25 minutes
Chilling time: 2 hours

IMPERIAL (METRIC)
1½ lb (680g) carrots
1½ pints (850ml) vegetable stock
Sea salt and freshly ground black
   pepper
2 tablespoonsful rose water

AMERICAN
1½ lb carrots
1 quart vegetable stock
Sea salt and freshly ground black
   pepper
2 tablespoonsful rose water

1. Trim, peel and wash the carrots and chop coarsely.
2. Place the carrots into a medium-sized saucepan and add the stock. Place over moderate heat, and bring to the boil. Reduce the heat and simmer for 20 minutes. Remove from the heat, season to taste and allow to cool.
3. Place the contents of the saucepan into a blender container and purée. Pour into a container, stir in the rose water and chill in the refrigerator for at least 2 hours.

CREAM OF SCAMPI SOUP

Serves 4

Preparation time: 10 minutes
Cooking time: 15 minutes
Chilling time: 2 hours

IMPERIAL (METRIC)
½ lb (225g) frozen scampi tails,
   defrosted
1 oz (30g) butter
1 pint (570ml) skimmed milk
Sea salt and freshly ground black
   pepper
¼ pint (140ml) single cream
2 tablespoonsful finely chopped
   parsley

AMERICAN
½ lb frozen Mediterranean shrimp
   tails, defrosted
2 tablespoonsful butter
2½ cups skim milk
Sea salt and freshly ground black
   pepper
⅔ cup light cream
2 tablespoonsful finely chopped
   parsley

1. Chop the scampi tails coarsely.
2. Melt the butter in a medium-sized saucepan, add the scampi and sauté gently for 5 minutes.
3. Add the milk, season to taste, return to the heat and bring to the boil. Reduce the heat and simmer for 3 minutes. Remove from the heat and allow to cool.
4. Place the scampi mixture and cream in a blender container and blend until smooth. Pour into a container, stir in the parsley and chill in the refrigerator for at least 2 hours.

4

SANDWICHES AND FILLINGS

The sandwich is the most common form of portable food, making its appearance in a packed school lunch or at more upmarket occasions such as the Ascot races.

Sandwiches can be the dullest of all picnic foods. However, prepared well and with some amount of imagination, they can be as good as more esoteric picnic fare. One of my favourite choices for a Mediterranean beach picnic was always thick sandwiches of crusty local bread, filled with tuna fish, capers and onions — they never failed to please.

To make a good sandwich, ensure that the filling is generous, but compact enough not to fall out of the bread, or so moist that the bread is turned into a milk pudding. It is good to combine different textures in a filling so that instead of being pap, it has plenty of crunch to it. One of the best and simplest of sandwiches is a good mixed salad, and one of the most satisfying combinations in that sort of sandwich is the mixture of butter and mayonnaise upon the palate.

Make sure the bread you use for sandwiches is fresh and of high quality; sandwiches made from sliced, refined white bread might just as well be thrown to the seagulls. Also take care that sandwiches, once made, are wrapped and put into a container. There must never be a suspicion of staleness: the problem which affects shop sandwiches and makes them so undesirable. The choice of bread is yours. Whether you choose wholemeal, brown, granary or white is a matter of personal preference, since excellent sandwiches can be made with any type of good bread. I would personally choose to have both wholemeal and white breads for a picnic. A very popular American sandwich that is gaining favour here is the 'club' or triple-decker sandwich. The classic is a standard BLT (bacon, lettuce and tomato to the uninitiated) between two slices of toast, with the 'upper deck' containing sliced chicken or turkey, more lettuce and Russian or Thousand Island dressing (a combination of mayonnaise, pickle relish and tomato ketchup). Since we are excluding meat from this book, one might try to construct a modified club sandwich using two fish fillings with appropriate vegetables and sauces or vegetable fillings or any combination of the recipes suggested in this chapter that appeal to you, plus the bread of your choice.

Whether you decide to spread the bread with butter, margarine, a low fat spread, cheese or nothing at all is up to you, although a spread helps keep the filling from soaking through the bread. I would choose unsalted French butter for the flavour it imparts to the sandwich. One might argue that the flavour of polyunsaturated margarine is not going to matter much in a sandwich where the filling flavour is dominant — for example, anchovy or smoked mackerel paste — but I would disagree, since I feel that margarine tends to hinder taste rather than help it.

Sandwiches do not need a garnish, although they are often given one in restaurants. My belief is that the filling itself is the garnish and the band of colour between the slices of bread should look appealing. Therefore, when making the filling, some visual discretion should be used.

Giving guidelines for how many people the following sandwich fillings will serve is somewhat difficult without knowing whether the intention is for the sandwich to be the main part of the meal or the appetizer, but the following fillings are sufficient for one small loaf of bread.

There should be a rough ratio between strong filling flavours, which need to be thinly spread, and the thinness of the slice of bread. A thicker filling calls for a doorstep piece of bread.

FISH FILLINGS

ANCHOVY AND CUCUMBER FILLING

Preparation time: 10 minutes

IMPERIAL (METRIC)	AMERICAN
3 tins anchovies in olive oil	*3 cans anchovies in olive oil*
1 tablespoonful capers	*1 tablespoonful capers*
Freshly ground black pepper	*Freshly ground black pepper*
½ cucumber	*1 cucumber*

1. Place the anchovies and oil in a blender container. Add the capers and pepper to taste and blend to a purée.
2. Slice the cucumber thinly.
3. Spread the anchovy paste thinly over the bread and arrange the cucumber slices on top, then cover with another slice of bread.

CRAB AND EGG FILLING

Preparation time: 15 minutes

IMPERIAL (METRIC)	AMERICAN
2 small dressed crabs	*2 small crabs, cooked*
3 eggs, hard-boiled	*3 eggs, hard-cooked*
2 tablespoonsful mayonnaise	*2 tablespoonsful mayonnaise*

1. Extract the flesh from the crab bodies. Crack the claws and extract the flesh. In a bowl, mix together the brown and white crab meat.
2. Shell and mash the eggs and add to the crab.
3. Stir in enough mayonnaise to bind the ingredients together.
4. Spread generously on the bread.

PRAWN AND COLESLAW FILLING

Preparation time: 10 minutes

IMPERIAL (METRIC)	AMERICAN
1 lb (455g) unshelled prawns, cooked	*1 lb unshelled large shrimp, cooked*
6 oz (170g) coleslaw (page 120)	*¾ cup coleslaw (page 120)*

1. If the prawns are heads-on, remove the heads and squeeze the juices into a bowl. Add the coleslaw.
2. Shell the prawns and add to the coleslaw, mixing thoroughly.
3. Be generous with this filling.

SMOKED HADDOCK AND EGG FILLING

Preparation time: 10 minutes
Cooking time: 10 minutes

IMPERIAL (METRIC)
1 oz (30g) butter
1½ lb (680g) Finnan haddock
3 eggs, hard-boiled
Pinch of sea salt and lots of freshly
*   ground black pepper*

AMERICAN
2 tablespoonsful butter
1½ lb Finnan haddie
3 eggs, hard-cooked
Pinch of sea salt and lots of freshly
*   ground black pepper*

1. Melt the butter in a medium-sized saucepan over low heat and add the haddock. Cook gently for 10 minutes. Remove from the heat and allow to cool.
2. Remove the skin and bones from the fish and flake the flesh in a bowl, adding the buttery juices from the pan.
3. Shell and mash the eggs in a bowl, adding a pinch of salt and lots of pepper. Combine with the fish and mix well.
4. Be generous with this filling and try not to eat most of it before it goes into the sandwiches.

SMOKED SALMON AND CREAM CHEESE FILLING

I once knew a Church of England rector who economized on these sandwiches by making them out of smoked salmon pieces, which are a great deal cheaper. The result was disastrous and it is my belief that his economy was misplaced. Nevertheless, you do not need to use the best quality smoked salmon for sandwiches.

Preparation time: 10 minutes

IMPERIAL (METRIC)
1 onion, finely chopped
5 oz (140g) cream cheese
Lots of freshly ground black pepper
Butter to spread
1 lb (455g) smoked salmon, thinly
*   sliced*
Chopped fresh dillweed (optional)

AMERICAN
1 onion, finely chopped
5 oz cream cheese (slightly more than
*   half an 8-oz package)*
Lots of freshly ground black pepper
Butter to spread
1 lb smoked salmon, thinly sliced
Chopped fresh dill (optional)

1. In a small bowl, mix the onion with the cheese and pepper.
2. Spread the bread with the finest quality butter, then with the cheese mixture. Place a thin layer of salmon over the cheese and if you wish, grind some additional pepper over. Place the dillweed, if using, over the salmon, and cover with another slice of buttered bread.

SMOKED MACKEREL PÂTÉ AND ONION FILLING

Buy smoked mackerel with care. If it is too large, it will be too oily. A medium-sized mackerel should be no longer than 12 inches (30cm). When you are skinning it, if there are any signs of white fat, remove it from the flesh as it will make the pâté too rich.

Preparation time: minimal

IMPERIAL (METRIC)	AMERICAN
1 medium-sized smoked mackerel, skinned and filleted	*1 medium-sized smoked mackerel, skinned and filleted*
1 tablespoonful lemon juice	*1 tablespoonful lemon juice*
1 tablespoonful horseradish sauce	*1 tablespoonful horseradish sauce*
2 tablespoonsful chopped parsley	*2 tablespoonsful chopped parsley*
1 onion, finely chopped	*1 onion, finely chopped*
Freshly ground black pepper	*Freshly ground black pepper*
1 onion, thinly sliced	*1 onion, thinly sliced*

1. Flake the mackerel flesh into a bowl.
2. Add all the remaining ingredients except for the sliced onion and mix into a rough paste; there is no need for it to be too smooth, since, in my opinion, it tastes better rough.
3. Spread the mackerel pâté on the bread and top with the sliced onion.

SMOKED TROUT AND WALNUT FILLING

Preparation time: minimal

IMPERIAL (METRIC)	AMERICAN
2 smoked trout, skinned and filleted	*2 smoked trout, skinned and filleted*
1 tablespoonful lemon juice	*1 tablespoonful lemon juice*
1 tablespoonful soured cream	*1 tablespoonful sour cream*
3 oz (85g) walnuts, broken	*¾ cup broken walnuts*
Pinch of sea salt and lots of freshly ground black pepper	*Pinch of sea salt and lots of freshly ground black pepper*
1 onion, thinly sliced	*1 onion, thinly sliced*

1. Flake the trout flesh into a bowl.
2. Add all of the remaining ingredients, except for the sliced onion and mix into a rough paste.
3. Spread the mixture on the bread and top with the sliced onion.

TUNA AND CAPER FILLING

Preparation time: minimal

IMPERIAL (METRIC)
1 14-oz (395g) tin tuna in brine
2 tablespoonsful capers
1 bunch spring onions, finely
   chopped
2 tablespoonsful soured cream
Pinch of sea salt and lots of freshly
   ground black pepper

AMERICAN
14 oz canned tuna packed in water
2 tablespoonsful capers
1 bunch scallions, finely chopped
2 tablespoonsful sour cream
Pinch of sea salt and lots of freshly
   ground black pepper

1.   Drain the tuna thoroughly and flake the flesh into a large bowl.
2.   Add the remaining ingredients and mix well.

SARDINE AND TOMATO FILLING

Preparation time: 10 minutes

IMPERIAL (METRIC)
2 tins sardines in olive oil
1 tablespoonsful Meaux mustard
Sea salt and freshly ground black
   pepper
4 medium-sized tomatoes

AMERICAN
2 cans sardines in olive oil
1 tablespoonsful Meaux mustard
Sea salt and freshly ground black
   pepper
4 medium-sized tomatoes

1.   Drain the sardines and remove their backbones. Tip into a bowl.
2.   Add the mustard and seasoning and mash into a thick purée.
3.   Slice the tomatoes thinly.
4.   Spread the sardine purée on the bread and cover with the tomato slices.

KIPPER PÂTÉ AND COURGETTES

Preparation time: 10 minutes
Cooking time: 5 minutes

IMPERIAL (METRIC)
2 pairs undyed kippers
1 oz (30g) butter, softened
1 tablespoonful lemon juice
Freshly ground black pepper
3 small courgettes

AMERICAN
2 pairs undyed fresh kippered
  herrings
2 tablespoonsful butter, softened
1 tablespoonful lemon juice
Freshly ground black pepper
3 small zucchini

1. Place the two pairs of kippers into a frying pan in a sandwich (so that one pair is skin-side down and the other is skin-side up). Pour in a little boiling water, cover the pan tightly and steam over moderate heat for about 5 minutes, until the flesh is tender. Remove from the heat and allow to cool.
2. Flake the kipper flesh into a bowl, discarding the skin and all the bones. Add the remaining ingredients except for the courgettes and mix thoroughly.
3. Cut the courgettes into wafer-thin slices.
4. Spread the kipper pâté on the bread and top with the courgette slices.

VEGETABLE FILLINGS

ALFALFA SPROUT AND MOZZARELLA FILLING
Preparation time: minimal

Alfalfa sprouts can now be bought in wholefood shops, but they are very easily grown at home and it is much cheaper to do it yourself.

Sprout the seeds in a container or jam jar; it will take five days before they can be harvested and eaten.

Sprouts are a sort of miracle food — they are very high in protein, vitamins and minerals. They also happen to be amazingly delicious, having a slight peppery flavour and a lovely crunchy texture.

Real mozzarella cheese comes wrapped in paper and is stored in brine. To use, the cheese should be drained, then sliced. Real mozzarella is far superior to the processed vacuum-packed cheese which has no flavour and the texture of plastic.

To make this sandwich filling, slice the mozzarella thinly and place it on the bread. Spread the cheese with a little home-made mustard or chutney and then cover with a generous portion of alfalfa sprouts.

SALAD AND FETA CHEESE FILLING

This filling is based on the ingredients for a traditional Greek Salad.

Cut the olives, tomatoes, cucumbers and Feta cheese more thinly than you would for a salad and slice or shred the lettuce. Moisten with a little home-made mayonnaise to bind the salad together and spread the bread with unsalted French butter.

This is also an excellent filling for pitta bread.

MUSHROOM AND EGG FILLING

Preparation time: 10 minutes
Cooking time: 5 minutes

IMPERIAL (METRIC)
½ lb (225g) mushrooms
1 oz (30g) butter
4 eggs, hard-boiled
½ teaspoonful Tabasco sauce
Sea salt and freshly ground black
    pepper

AMERICAN
½ lb mushrooms
2 tablespoonful butter
4 eggs, hard-cooked
½ teaspoonful Tabasco sauce
Sea salt and freshly ground black
    pepper

1. Slice the mushrooms thinly.
2. Melt the butter in a medium-sized saucepan and add the mushrooms. Cook over high heat, stirring constantly, until the juices are absorbed and the mushrooms are just tender, about 5 minutes. Remove from the heat and tip into a bowl.
3. Shell and mash the eggs and add to the mushrooms with the Tabasco sauce and seasoning. Mix to a chunky purée.

SCRAMBLED EGG AND PEPPER FILLING

Cooking time: 5 minutes

IMPERIAL (METRIC)
1 oz (30g) butter
4 eggs, beaten
2 green peppers, deseeded and
    chopped
Sea salt and freshly ground black
    pepper
2 tablespoonful home-made tartare
    sauce

AMERICAN
2 tablespoonful butter
4 eggs, beaten
2 green peppers, seeded and chopped
Sea salt and freshly ground black
    pepper
2 tablespoonful home-made tartare
    sauce

1. Melt the butter in a frying pan over moderate heat. Pour in the eggs, green peppers and seasoning and stir with a fork until the eggs are cooked. Remove from the heat and tip the mixture into a bowl.
2. Break up the mixture with a fork. Spread on bread and top with tartare sauce.

MISO AND TAHINI FILLING

This is an amazingly delicious spread and exceptionally high in nutritional value, although it is not for the faint-hearted as it has a rather strong flavour.

Simply mix one part miso (fermented bean paste) to two parts tahini (sesame paste). No seasoning is necessary.

BEAN PURÉE AND TOMATO FILLING

Soaking time: 1 hour
Preparation time: 5 minutes
Cooking time: 40–50 minutes

IMPERIAL (METRIC)
4 oz (115g) flageolet beans, soaked for
*   1 hour*
3 cloves garlic, crushed
1 onion, peeled
1 bay leaf
2 oz (55g) butter, softened
Sea salt and freshly ground black
*   pepper*
Generous handful of parsley, finely
*   chopped*
4 medium-sized tomatoes, thinly
*   sliced*

AMERICAN
²/₃ cup navy beans, soaked for 1 hour
3 cloves garlic, crushed
1 onion, peeled
1 bay leaf
4 tablespoonsful butter, softened
Sea salt and freashly ground black
*   pepper*
Generous handful of parsley, finely
*   chopped*
4 medium-sized tomatoes, thinly
*   sliced*

1. Drain the beans and place in a medium-sized saucepan with the garlic, onion and bay leaf. Cover with enough water to rise 1 inch (2.5cm) above the beans and bring to the boil over moderate heat. Reduce the heat and simmer for 40–50 minutes, until the beans are tender. Remove from the heat, drain thoroughly and discard the bay leaf.
2. Place the contents of the saucepan into a blender container, add the butter and seasoning and reduce to a thick purée. Spoon into a bowl and mix in the parsley.
3. Spread the bean purée on bread and cover with thinly sliced tomatoes.

AUBERGINE AND SESAME FILLING

Preparation time: 5 minutes
Cooking time: 3 hours
Chilling time: 30 minutes

IMPERIAL (METRIC)	AMERICAN
2 medium-sized aubergines	*2 medium-sized eggplants*
Oil	*Oil*
2 oz (55g) butter, softened	*4 tablespoonsful butter, softened*
2 tablespoonsful soured cream	*2 tablespoonsful sour cream*
Sea salt and freshly ground black pepper	*Sea salt and freshly ground black pepper*
2 oz (55g) sesame seeds, toasted	*6 tablespoonsful sesame seeds, toasted*

1. Heat the oven to 300°F/150°C (Gas Mark 2).
2. Oil the skins of the aubergines, place on a baking sheet and bake for 3 hours until the flesh is soft. Remove from the oven and allow to cool.
3. When the aubergines are cool enough to handle, cut them in half lengthways and scoop out all the flesh.
4. Place the aubergine flesh in a blender container with the butter and soured cream and season generously. Blend to a purée.
5. Tip the aubergine mixture into a bowl and stir in the sesame seeds. Cover and chill in the refrigerator for 30 minutes, or until it has a spreadable consistency.

SAVOURY CHEESE FILLING

Preparation time: minimal

IMPERIAL (METRIC)	AMERICAN
5 oz (140g) cottage cheese	*²/₃ cup cottage cheese*
5 oz (140g) cream cheese	*5 oz cream cheese (slightly more than half of an 8-oz package)*
Generous handful of parsley, finely chopped	*Generous handful of parsley, finely chopped*
3 small gherkins, finely chopped	*3 small gherkins, finely chopped*
1 tablespoonful capers	*1 tablespoonful capers*
1 teaspoonful green peppercorns	*1 teaspoonful green peppercorns*
Pinch of sea salt and freshly ground black pepper	*Pinch of sea salt and freshly ground black pepper*

1. Place all the ingredients in a large bowl and mash together well.
2. Use as a spread.

ASPARAGUS AND EGG FILLING

Preparation time: 10 minutes
Cooking time: 6–12 minutes

IMPERIAL (METRIC)	AMERICAN
1 lb (455g) asparagus	*1 lb asparagus*
2 oz (55g) butter, softened	*4 tablespoonsful butter, softened*
Sea salt and freshly ground black pepper	*Sea salt and freshly ground black pepper*
3 eggs, hard-boiled	*3 eggs, hard-cooked*

1. Wash the asparagus and place upright in an asparagus steamer. Steam for 12 minutes, or until just tender. Alternatively, boil in very little water for 6 minutes. Remove from the heat and allow to cool.
2. Slice off the asparagus tips and reserve. Scrape the flesh from the stalks into a blender container, discarding the fibrous ends. Add the butter and seasoning and blend to a purée.
3. Place the asparagus purée in a bowl. Shell and mash the eggs and add to the asparagus. Stir in the reserved asparagus tips.
4. Use as a spread.

CELERY AND BLUE CHEESE FILLING

Preparation time: minimal

IMPERIAL (METRIC)	AMERICAN
Hearts of 2 heads of celery, plus the leaves, all finely chopped	*Hearts of 2 heads of celery, plus the leaves, all finely chopped*
4 oz (115g) blue cheese (Roquefort, Stilton, Fourme d'Ambert or Beenleigh Blue)	*4 oz blue cheese (Roquefort, Stilton, Gorgonzola or Danish Blue)*

1. This spread is simplicity itself. Combine the celery and cheese thoroughly until they become a thick, chunky mixture.

5

PÂTÉS, TERRINES, MOUSSES AND MOULDS

Pâtés, terrines, mousses and moulds are all related to each other in that their preparation involves making a purée. All of the recipes in this chapter are served cold and can be packed easily.

The pâtés and terrines are meant to be unmoulded, then wrapped in cling film and packed, but the mousses can be made in a plastic bowl (that has a tightly fitting lid), chilled in the refrigerator to set and spooned out at the picnic. Because of this method of preparation, it is not really worthwhile to make a layered mousse, which would ordinarily be cut to display its variously coloured layers.

Actually, the difference between a mousse and a terrine may be difficult to pin down. Basically, a mousse is very light in texture, with stiffly whisked egg whites folded in, while a terrine can have the texture of a mousse, but with the addition of vegetables and/or fish which patterns it. Terrines can also be made in various layers. They are attractive and enticing to look at and have become a speciality of cooks who wish to impress their guests. Unfortunately, in some instances, they have become too bland in flavour. This problem can be easily solved by choosing mixtures flavoured with herbs, spices and spirits. Always check the taste before cooking the purées.

Another dilemma is what ingredient to use to make these dishes set fairly firm. The choices are: eggs and cream; gelatine; agar-agar; a gelatinous fish stock; or a jelly made from carragheen. The solution depends on your own dietary restrictions. If you are limiting the amount of fat in your diet, eggs and cream should be avoided. If you are a vegetarian purist, you will avoid gelatine. There is also the question of whether you eat fish or not. Personally, I am watchful on the fat issue, but do not avoid it completely, and as I explained earlier in this book, I am ambivalent regarding the other matters. If you should choose agar-agar as your setting agent, it has to be boiled for a few minutes so that it becomes soluble and melts completely.

Pastes and pâtés are far easier to make, and there is a wide choice as to what they can contain. Most pastes and pâtés could not be made easily before the advent of the electric blender.

Pâtés
See the chapter on sandwiches and fillings. Refrigerate the pâtés for several hours. Use as a spread.

TERRINES

When using fish in terrines, buy the varieties that are high in gelatine content, such as monkfish (lotte), brill, Dover sole, rock salmon (and other members of the shark family), skate, halibut and turbot. Buy the fish whole and make a stock from the head and bones. Then sieve and discard the bones and scraps. This liquid will jell when it cools. See the stock-making instructions on page 102 for more details.

CRAB AND COURGETTE TERRINE

Serves 6
Preparation time: 15 minutes
Cooking time: 15 minutes
Chilling time: 24 hours

IMPERIAL (METRIC)	AMERICAN
2 small carrots, grated	*2 small carrots, grated*
½ lb (140ml) baby courgettes, grated	*½ lb baby zucchini, grated*
2 dressed crabs	*2 crabs, cooked*
Generous handful of parsley, chopped	*Generous handful of parsley, chopped*
¼ pint (140ml) reduced fish stock	*⅔ cup reduced fish stock (see recipe,*
(see recipe, point 2, page 102)	*point 2, page 102)*
2 teaspoonsful agar-agar flakes	*2 teaspoonsful agar-agar flakes*
3 fl oz (90ml) brandy	*3 fl oz brandy*
Sea salt and freshly ground black	*Sea salt and freshly ground black*
pepper	*pepper*

1. Place the carrots and courgettes in separate bowls. Pour boiling water over both and leave for 2 minutes. Drain thoroughly and pat dry.
2. Extract the flesh from the bodies of the crabs. Crack the claws and extract the flesh. Add both the white and brown crab meat to the carrots and mix well. Add the parsley to the courgettes and mix well.
3. Heat the fish stock and add the agar-agar; bring to the boil, then reduce the heat and simmer for 10 minutes. Remove from the heat and add the brandy. Divide the stock between the carrots and courgettes, season and mix well.
4. Line a terrine or bread tin with buttered aluminium foil, large enough for two pieces to protude over the sides. Place a layer of the carrot-crab mixture in the base of the terrine, then a layer of the courgette mixture. Continue layering until both mixtures are used up. Level the top of the terrine with the back of a knife and chill in the refrigerator for 24 hours.
5. To unmould, gently pull the two pieces of foil to loosen. Place a serving plate on top of the terrine, then reserve so that the plate is underneath. Slide the mould off and carefully remove the foil.

WHITE FISH AND LAVER TERRINE

Laver is the most popular of all sea vegetables. It can be bought in tins from The Drangway Restaurant, 66 Wind Street, Swansea, Wales. Delicatessens, health food and wholefood shops also stock laver. If you live in Wales, you are fortunate, as you can buy laver (called laver bread) in the markets. It is inexpensive and highly nutritious.

Serves 6
Preparation time: 15 minutes
Cooking time: 40 minutes
Chilling time: 24 hours

IMPERIAL (METRIC)
2 lb (900g) whole white fish (use a
  mixture chosen from the varieties
  listed above)
1½ pints (850ml) water
2 bay leaves
1 bouquet garni
¼ pint (140ml) dry sherry
2 tablespoonsful capers
4 oz (115g) Gruyère cheese, grated
Sea salt and freshly ground black
  pepper
1 tin laver

AMERICAN
2 lb whole white fish (use a mixture
  chosen from the varieties listed
  above)
1 quart water
2 bay leaves
1 bouquet garni
²/3 cup dry sherry
2 tablespoonsful capers
1 cup grated Gruyère cheese
Sea salt and freshly ground black
  pepper
1 can laver

1. Skin and fillet the fish, reserving the bones and heads. Set the fillets aside. Place the bones and heads in a large saucepan with the water, bay leaves and bouquet garni. Place over moderate heat, bring to a boil and boil for 30 minutes. During the last 5 minutes of cooking, place the fish fillets over the bones and lightly poach. Remove from the heat.
2. Remove the fish fillets to a bowl and reserve. Sieve the liquid from the bones and scraps into a saucepan. Discard bones and scraps. Place the liquid over high heat and reduce to ¼ pint/140ml/2/3 cup, then add the sherry. Remove from the heat.
3. Add the capers, half the cheese and half the stock to the bowl containing the fish fillets. Mix thoroughly. Season to taste.
4. Turn the laver into another bowl. Add the remaining cheese and stock and mix well. Season to taste.
5. Line a terrine or bread tin with buttered aluminium foil, large enough for two pieces to protrude over the sides. Place a layer of the fish mixture in the base of the terrine, then a layer of the laver mixture. Continue layering until both mixtures are used up. Level the terrine with the back of a knife and chill in the refrigerator for 24 hours.
6. To unmould, gently pull the two pieces of foil to loosen. Place a serving plate on top of the terrine, then invert so that the plate is underneath. Slide the mould off and carefully remove the foil.

Variation:
White Fish and Spinach Terrine
Follow the instructions above, but substitute spinach purée for the laver. Add 1 tablespoonful green peppercorns to the spinach mixture and 2 tablespoonsful pistachio nuts to the fish mixture. Omit the capers.

SMOKED HADDOCK AND MUSHROOM TERRINE

Serves 4-6

Preparation time: 20 minutes
Baking time: 30-40 minutes
Standing time: 10 minutes

IMPERIAL (METRIC)	AMERICAN
2 lb (900g) Finnan haddock	*2 lb Finnan haddie*
Freshly ground black pepper	*Freshly ground black pepper*
2 eggs	*2 eggs*
½ pint (285ml) single cream	*1¼ cups light cream*
1 oz (30g) butter	*2 tablespoonsful butter*
½ lb (225g) mushrooms, thinly sliced	*½ lb mushrooms, thinly sliced*
Sea salt	*Sea salt*

1. Preheat the oven to 425°F/220°C (Gas Mark 7).
2. Scrape all the flesh from the haddock into a bowl, ensuring that you have removed all the bones, and season generously with pepper. Whisk one of the eggs and add to the haddock with half the cream. Mix thoroughly.
3. Melt the butter in a medium-sized saucepan and sauté the mushrooms until soft. Remove from the heat, tip into a blender container and blend to a chunky purée. Pour into a clean bowl, add the remaining egg and cream and mix well. Season to taste.
4. Butter a terrine dish. Make alternate layers of the fish and mushrooms until both mixtures are used up.
5. Place the terrine in a bain-marie or larger ovenproof dish, pour boiling water into the dish halfway up the sides of the terrine and bake for 30–40 minutes. Remove from the oven and leave to settle for 10 minutes, then unmould.

GARDEN PEA TERRINE

The taste of fresh garden peas is one of the most sublime delights of summer. (Unfortunately, the frozen pea, with its chemical additives, has cast a blight over our palates.) This recipe is in celebration of the garden pea.

Serves 4–6
Preparation time: 10 minutes
Cooking time: 10 minutes
Baking time: 30–40 minutes
Standing time: 10 minutes

IMPERIAL (METRIC)	AMERICAN
3 lb (1.4kg) garden peas in their pods	*3 lb garden peas in their pods*
Sea salt	*Sea salt*
2 eggs	*2 eggs*
½ pint (285ml) single cream	*1¼ cups light cream*
Freshly ground black pepper	*Freshly ground black pepper*
2 baby courgettes	*2 baby zucchini*

1. Preheat the oven to 425°F/220°C (Gas Mark 7).
2. Pod the peas and cook in a medium-sized saucepan in very little salted water until tender, about 5 minutes. Remove from the heat.
3. Reserve 2 tablespoonsful peas and place the remainder in a blender container with the eggs, cream and seasoning and blend to a purée.
4. Slice the courgettes lengthways, then into small dice. Place in a steamer basket inside a small saucepan containing a little water. Cover and steam over moderate heat for 3–4 minutes. Remove from the heat and allow to cool, then add to the pea purée, stirring until well distributed.
5. Butter a terrine dish and pour in the purée. Place the terrine in a bain-marie or larger ovenproof dish, pour boiling water into the dish halfway up the sides of the terrine and bake for 30–40 minutes. Remove from the oven and leave to settle for 10 minutes, then unmould.

MOUSSES

AUBERGINE AND CARROT MOUSSE

Serves 6

Baking time: 2 hours
Preparation time: 10–15 minutes
Cooking time: 10 minutes
Chilling time: 24 hours

IMPERIAL (METRIC)	AMERICAN
2 large aubergines	*2 large eggplants*
Olive oil	*Olive oil*
1 lb (455g) carrots, roughly chopped	*1 lb carrots, roughly chopped*
2 oz (55g) butter	*4 tablespoonsful butter*
1 teaspoonful crushed cumin seeds	*1 teaspoonful crushed cumin seeds*
1 teaspoonful crushed coriander seeds	*1 teaspoonful crushed coriander seeds*
3 cloves garlic, crushed	*3 cloves garlic, crushed*
3 eggs, separated	*3 eggs, separated*
Sea salt and freshly ground black pepper	*Sea salt and freshly ground black pepper*

1. Set the oven temperature to 275°F/140°C (Gas Mark 1). Place the aubergines in a baking dish, oil the skins and bake for about 2 hours, or until the flesh is soft. Set aside to cool.
2. Place the carrots in a medium-sized saucepan with very little lightly salted water and cook over moderate heat until tender, about 10 minutes. Remove from the heat and mash to a thick purée.
3. Melt the butter in a clean medium-sized saucepan. Add the cumin, coriander, garlic and carrots and mix thoroughly. Remove from the heat.
4. Scrape all the aubergine flesh into the carrot purée, stir in the egg yolks and mix well.
5. Whisk the egg whites until stiff but not dry. Turn the carrot and aubergine mixture into a bowl, fold in the egg whites and place in the coolest part of the refrigerator and chill for 24 hours.

AVOCADO AND WATERCRESS MOUSSE

Serves 4–6
Preparation time: 15 minutes
Chilling time: 12–24 hours

IMPERIAL (METRIC)	AMERICAN
3 large ripe avocados	*3 large ripe avocados*
½ pint (285ml) smetana	*1¼ cups low-fat soured cream*
1 tablespoonful lime juice	*1 tablespoonful lime juice*
1 clove garlic, crushed	*1 clove garlic, crushed*
Sea salt and freshly ground black	*Sea salt and freshly ground black*
* pepper*	* pepper*
1 bunch watercress	*1 bunch watercress*
2 egg whites	*2 egg whites*

1. Peel and stone the avocados and scrape the avocado flesh into a blender container. Add the smetana, lime juice, garlic and seasoning and blend to a smooth purée.
2. Remove the watercress stalks and discard. Finely chop the leaves and add to the avocado purée. Blend again to incorporate the watercress evenly. Pour into a bowl.
3. Whisk the egg whites until stiff but not dry and fold into the avocado purée. Place in the coolest part of the refrigerator and chill for 12–24 hours.

TOMATO AND BASIL MOUSSE

Serves 6
Preparation time: 15 minutes
Cooking time: 15 minutes
Chilling time: 12–24 hours

IMPERIAL (METRIC)	AMERICAN
3 lb (1.4kg) ripe tomatoes	*3 lb ripe tomatoes*
3 cloves garlic, crushed	*3 cloves garlic, crushed*
3 fl oz (90ml) sherry	*3 fl oz sherry*
Sea salt and freshly ground black	*Sea salt and freshly ground black*
* pepper*	* pepper*
1 tablespoonful agar-agar flakes	*1 tablespoonful agar-agar flakes*
Generous bunch of basil	*Generous bunch of basil*

1. Puncture the tomatoes through their skins. Place in a large saucepan with the garlic, sherry and seasoning. Bring gently to the boil over moderate heat, reduce the heat and simmer for 10 minutes. Remove from the heat.
2. Meanwhile, place the agar-agar in a small saucepan with a little water, bring to the boil over moderate heat, reduce the heat and simmer for 10 minutes, until the agar-agar is completely dissolved. Remove from the heat.
3. Place the tomato mixture in a blender container and blend to a thick purée. Sieve to discard the skin and seeds and pour the tomato purée into a bowl.
4. Finely chop the basil leaves and mix into the tomato purée. Add the agar-agar and mix thoroughly.
5. Chill in the refrigerator for 12–24 hours.

MOULDS

The following recipes can either be poured into individual ramekins or one 2½ pint/1.4 litre/1½ quart mould or soufflé dish.

CABBAGE AND WALNUT MOULD

Serves 4–6

Preparation time:	10 minutes
Cooking time:	5 minutes
Baking time:	30–40 minutes
Standing time:	10 minutes

IMPERIAL (METRIC)
2 oz (55g) butter
1 small cabbage, finely chopped
  (Reserve several outer leaves to line
  the mould)
4 oz (115g) walnuts, chopped
½ lb (225g) cottage cheese
4 eggs, well beaten
Sea salt and freshly ground black
  pepper

AMERICAN
4 tablespoonsful butter
1 small cabbage, finely chopped
  (Reserve several outer leaves to line
  the mould)
1 cup chopped walnuts
½ lb cottage cheese
4 eggs, well beaten
Sea salt and freshly ground black
  pepper

1. Preheat the oven to 425°F/220°C (Gas Mark 7).
2. Melt the butter in a large saucepan with a tightly fitting lid. Add the cabbage and sauté for 5 minutes, or until the cabbage is just tender. Remove from the heat and stir in the walnuts, cheese, eggs and seasoning. Mix thoroughly.
3. Butter individual ramekins or a 2½ pint/1.4 litre/1½ quart mould and line the base and sides with the reserved cabbage leaves, leaving enough overlapping at the top to enclose the filling completely.
4. Pour the cabbage mixture into the ramekins or mould. Fold down the cabbage leaves, cover with buttered greaseproof paper and place the mould in a larger ovenproof dish. Pour enough boiling water into the dish to come halfway up the sides of the mould and bake for 30–40 minutes. Remove from the oven and leave to settle for 10 minutes before unmoulding.

Opposite: Avocado and Onion Flan (page 115).
Overleaf: A Cold Day at the Races (pages 38 to 41).

SPINACH AND LEEK MOULD

Serves 4-6

Preparation time:	15 minutes
Cooking time:	6–8 minutes
Baking time:	30–40 minutes
Standing time:	10 minutes

IMPERIAL (METRIC)	AMERICAN
2 lb (900g) leeks	*2 lb leeks*
2 oz (55g) butter	*4 tablespoonsful butter*
4 eggs	*4 eggs*
½ pint (285ml) single cream	*1¼ cups light cream*
2 tablespoonsful shelled pistachio nuts	*2 tablespoonsful shelled pistachio nuts*
Sea salt and freshly ground black pepper	*Sea salt and freshly ground black pepper*
Several spinach leaves to line the moulds, blanched until wilted	*Several spinach leaves to line the moulds, blanched until wilted*

1. Preheat the oven to 425°F/220°C (Gas Mark 7).
2. Trim, clean and slice the leeks finely.
3. Melt the butter in a medium-sized saucepan and add the leeks. Cover and cook over low heat for 6-8 minutes, or until just tender. Remove from the heat and leave to cool.
4. Place the contents of the saucepan into a blender container. Add the eggs and cream and blend to a thick purée. Stir in the pistachio nuts and seasoning.
5. Butter individual ramekins or a 2½ pint/1.4 litre/1½ quart mould and line the base and sides with the spinach leaves, leaving enough overlapping at the top to enclose the filling completely.
6. Pour the leek purée into the ramekins or mould. Fold down the spinach leaves, cover with buttered greaseproof paper and place the mould(s) in a larger ovenproof dish. Pour enough boiling water into the dish to come halfway up the sides of the mould and bake for 30-40 minutes. Remove from the oven and leave to settle for 10 minutes before unmoulding.

Opposite: Smoked Haddock and Spinach Moulds (page 91).

GREEN PEA AND ASPARAGUS MOULD

Serves 4–6

Preparation time:	30 minutes
Cooking time:	15 minutes
Baking time:	30–40 minutes
Standing time:	10 minutes

IMPERIAL (METRIC)
*1 lb (455g) fresh garden peas in their
  pods
1 lb (455g) asparagus
½ pint (285ml) single cream
3 eggs
Sea salt and freshly ground black
  pepper
Several large lettuce leaves to line*

AMERICAN
*1 lb fresh garden peas in their pods
1 lb asparagus
1¼ cups light cream
3 eggs
Sea salt and freshly ground black
  pepper
Several large lettuce leaves to line*

1. Preheat the oven to 425°F/220°C (Gas Mark 7).
2. Pod the peas and place in a medium-sized saucepan. Bring to the boil over gentle heat and cook until tender, about 5 minutes. Remove from the heat and drain well.
3. Trim the asparagus and boil or steam until just tender. Remove from the heat, discard the fibrous ends, cut off the tips and set aside.
4. Place the peas, asparagus stalks, cream, eggs and seasoning in a blender container and blend to a purée. Stir in the reserved asparagus tips.
5. Butter individual ramekins or a 2½ pint/1.4 litre/1½ quart mould and line with the lettuce leaves, leaving enough overlapping at the top to enclose the filling completely.
6. Pour the pea and asparagus purée into the ramekins or mould. Fold down the lettuce leaves, cover with buttered greaseproof paper and place the mould(s) in a larger ovenproof dish. Pour enough boiling water into the dish to come halfway up the sides of the mould and bake for 30–40 minutes. Remove from the oven and leave to settle for 10 minutes before unmoulding.

SMOKED HADDOCK AND SPINACH MOULD

Serves 4–6

Preparation time: 15 minutes
Cooking time: 15 minutes
Baking time: 30–40 minutes
Standing time: 10 minutes

IMPERIAL (METRIC)	AMERICAN
2 oz (55g) butter	*4 tablespoonsful butter*
2 lb (900g) Finnan haddock	*2 lb Finnan haddie*
1 lb (455g) spinach (Reserve several outer leaves to line the mould)	*1 lb spinach (Reserve several outer leaves to line the mould)*
2 eggs	*2 eggs*
2 tablespoonsful green peppercorns	*2 tablespoonsful green peppercorns*
½ pint (285ml) single cream	*1¼ cups light cream*
Sea salt and freshly ground black pepper	*Sea salt and freshly ground black pepper*

1. Preheat the oven to 425°F/220°C (Gas Mark 7).
2. Melt half the butter in a frying pan large enough to accommodate the haddock over moderate heat. Cook the haddock lightly until the flesh flakes, about 5 minutes. Remove from the heat and allow to cool.
3. Blanch the reserved spinach leaves and set aside.
4. Melt the remaining butter in a medium-sized saucepan and add the remaining spinach. Cook over moderate heat until it is reduced in bulk by two-thirds. Increase the heat to drive off the remaining moisture, then remove from the heat and chop roughly with a wooden spoon.
5. Remove and discard the skin and bones from the haddock; place the flesh in a bowl and add one beaten egg, the green peppercorns and half the cream. Season to taste and mix well.
6. Place the spinach in another bowl, add the remaining beaten egg and cream, season to taste and mix thoroughly.
7. Butter individual ramekins or a 2½ pint/1.4 litres/1½ quart mould and line with the reserved spinach leaves, leaving enough overlapping at the top to enclose the filling completely.
8. Spread half the haddock mixture in the base of the mould(s), cover with the spinach mixture and top with the remaining haddock mixture. Fold down the spinach leaves, cover with buttered greaseproof paper and place the mould(s) in a larger ovenproof dish. Pour enough boiling water into the dish to come halfway up the sides of the mould and bake for 30–40 minutes. Remove from the oven and leave to settle for 10 minutes before unmoulding.

SCAMPI AND CARROT MOULD

Serves 4–6

Preparation time:	15 minutes
Cooking time:	10 minutes
Baking time:	30–40 minutes
Standing time:	10 minutes

IMPERIAL (METRIC)	AMERICAN
1 lb (455g) baby carrots	*1 lb baby carrots*
1½ lb (680g) frozen scampi tails, defrosted	*1½ lb frozen scampi tails, defrosted or use fresh if available*
½ pint (285 ml) single cream	*1¼ cups light cream*
3 eggs, beaten	*3 eggs, beaten*
2 tablespoonsful chopped dillweed or *fennel*	*2 tablespoonsful chopped dill* or *fennel*
Sea salt and freshly ground black pepper	*Sea salt and freshly ground black pepper*
Several large lettuce leaves, blanched until limp	*Several large lettuce leaves, blanched until limp*

1. Preheat the oven to 425°F/220°C (Gas Mark 7).
2. Trim, scrape and chop the carrots. Place in a medium-sized saucepan with very little water and cook over moderate heat until tender. Remove from the heat, drain well, then mash coarsely.
3. Place the scampi tails in a bowl. Add the carrots, cream, eggs and dillweed or fennel and season to taste.
4. Butter individual ramekins or a 2½ pint/1.4 litre/1½ quart mould and line with the lettuce leaves, leaving enough overlapping at the top to enclose the filling completely.
5. Spread the scampi and carrot mixture evenly in the mould(s). Fold down the lettuce leaves, cover with buttered greaseproof paper and place the mould(s) in a larger ovenproof dish. Pour enough boiling water into the dish to come halfway up the sides of the mould and bake for 30–40 minutes. Remove from the oven and leave to settle for 10 minutes before unmoulding.

6

STUFFED BREADS AND PIZZA

A loaf of bread in all its shapes, forms and sizes is an edible container for an infinite variety of stuffings.

The provençal *Pan Bagna* is a loaf cut in half, its inside hollowed out, filled with tomatoes, garlic, anchovies, olives and lettuce, soaked in good olive oil and wine vinegar, weighted and left overnight. I once made this for two travellers returning to London from Greece. They grandly refused their airline food and proceeded to unwrap the foil of their *Pan Bagna*. They told me afterwards that the cabin of the plane filled with the intense aroma of garlic and that other travellers edged away. However, you need not be as generous as I was with the garlic, and a modest French loaf will take kindly to this treatment.

Another possibility is to stuff home-made bread before baking. Any vegetable stuffing will suffice; cooked tomatoes, mushrooms or leeks can be placed inside the dough using the following technique. Place two-thirds of the bread dough in the tin, arrange the stuffing over it and cover with the remaining dough. Set the dough aside to prove for 1 hour, then bake in the normal way. (A provençal mixture of tomato, garlic and anchovy is particularly delicious.) The filling looks very attractive when the loaf is cut, but does have a tendency to fall out. However, there is no gustatory advantage to cutting a slice of baked bread and spreading the mixture on, so I prefer to put up with the former.

WHOLEMEAL LEEK LOAF

Makes one 2-lb (900g) loaf

Preparation time:	30 minutes
Standing time:	2 hours
Baking time:	40 minutes

IMPERIAL (METRIC)
1 lb (455g) wholemeal flour
1 teaspoonful sea salt
1 sachet micronized yeast
2 tablespoonsful olive oil
½ pint (270ml) warm water

AMERICAN
1 lb wholewheat flour
1 teaspoonful sea salt
1 package active dry yeast and 1
  teaspoonful sugar dissolved in ¼
  cup tepid water
2 tablespoonsful olive oil
1⅛ cups tepid water

STUFFING:
1 lb (455g) leeks
2 oz (55g) butter, softened
Sea salt and freshly ground black
  pepper
1 egg, beaten to glaze
Poppy seeds to sprinkle

STUFFING:
1 lb leeks
4 tablespoonsful butter, softened
Sea salt and freshly ground black
  pepper
1 egg, beaten to glaze
Poppy seeds to sprinkle

1. Read the general instructions for home-made bread on page 137.
2. In a bowl mix all of the dry ingredients together thoroughly, then add the oil and water (and ordinary dry yeast mixture, if using) and knead for 8–10 minutes, until the dough is elastic. Form into a ball, place back into the bowl, cover and allow to rise in a warm place, free from draughts, for 1 hour, until doubled in bulk.
3. Roll the dough out into a neat rectangle.
4. Clean, trim and chop the leeks finely. Mix with the softened butter and seasoning and place the stuffing in a column lengthways down the centre of the dough. With a sharp knife, cut both sides of the dough at 1-inch (2.5cm) intervals just up to the stuffing. Bring up one end to enclose the stuffing, then bring up the opposite end and tuck it under the first and press together to seal.
5. Grease a baking sheet, place the loaf on it and leave to rise for 1 hour.
6. About 15 minutes before baking, preheat the oven to 350°F/180°C (Gas Mark 5).
7. When ready to bake, brush the top of the loaf with the beaten egg and sprinkle with poppy seeds. Bake for 40 minutes. Remove from the oven and cool on a wire rack.

CROÛTES

Cut a large French stick into 2½-inch (6cm) thick slices. Cut a hollow from the centre of each slice about ½ inch (1.25cm) deep, leaving a rim of ¼ inch (.6cm) around the edge. Brush with olive oil and place in an oven preheated to 325°F/170°C (Gas Mark 3) for 10 minutes, or until they are just crisp and brown. Stuff with any of the sandwich fillings (pages 71–80) that would be suitable. Wrap individually with cling film.

PITTA POCKETS

Pitta bread is an excellent receptacle for stuffing. Use any of the sandwich fillings on pages 71–80, or fill with salad. In the Middle East, children eat stuffed bread as our children eat packets of crisps.

PIZZA

It is very easy to make your own pizza, and it also tends to travel well.

Serves 4–6
Preparation time: 20 minutes
Standing time: 2½ hours
Cooking time: 1 hour (can be done while dough is rising)
Baking time: 30 minutes

IMPERIAL (METRIC)	AMERICAN
Pizza base:	Pizza base:
½ lb (225g) unbleached strong white flour	2 cups unbleached white bread flour
½ teaspoonful salt	½ teaspoonful salt
½ oz (15g) fresh yeast	1 cake compressed yeast
2 tablespoonful warm milk	2 tablespoonful warm milk
1 egg, beaten	1 egg, beaten
2 tablespoonful olive oil	2 tablespoonful olive oil
2–3 tablespoonful warm water	2–3 tablespoonful warm water
Filling:	Filling:
2 onions	2 onions
1 green pepper	1 green pepper
2 tablespoonful olive oil	2 tablespoonful olive oil
5 cloves garlic, crushed	5 cloves garlic, crushed
1 teaspoonful dried oregano	1 teaspoonful dried oregano
14 oz (395g) tinned tomatoes	14 oz canned tomatoes
2 tablespoonful tomato purée	2 tablespoonful tomato paste
Sea salt and freshly ground black pepper	Sea salt and freshly ground black pepper
Garnish:	Garnish:
5 fresh tomatoes, sliced	5 fresh tomatoes, sliced
12 black olives, stoned	12 pitted black olives
2 tablespoonful capers	2 tablespoonful capers

1. Sift the flour and salt into a large bowl.
2. Crumble the yeast into a cup and pour over the warm milk. Stir and set aside until frothy, about 10 minutes.
3. Add the creamed yeast to the flour, then add the egg, oil and water. Stir well. Knead the dough until it is smooth and elastic, about 10 minutes. Form into a ball, place in a covered bowl and leave in a warm place free from draughts for about 2 hours, until doubled in bulk.
4. Meanwhile, make the filling. Slice the onions and deseed and slice the pepper.
5. Heat the olive oil in a medium-sized saucepan and add the sliced onions, pepper, garlic and oregano. Sauté gently for about 10 minutes, then add the tinned tomatoes. Increase the heat and simmer for 45 minutes, until the sauce is thick. Add the tomato purée, season to taste and cook for a further 5 minutes. Remove from the heat.

6. Preheat the oven to 425°F/220°C (Gas Mark 7). Oil a 12×14-inch (30×45cm) baking sheet.

7. Place the ball of risen dough in the centre of the baking sheet and smooth out, pressing and pulling the dough to the edges of the baking sheet. Form a small ridge of dough around the edges to enclose the filling. Leave to rest for 10 minutes.

8. Smear the filling over the dough and garnish with the fresh tomatoes, olives and capers. Leave to rest for a further 10 minutes.

9. Bake for 15 minutes, then decrease the oven temperature to 350°F/180°C (Gas Mark 4) and bake for a further 15 minutes.

7

PIES AND SAVOURY PASTRIES

Pies and pastries of various types appear at so many picnics for good reason. They have become part of the enjoyment of eating al fresco because they have certain advantages: they pack and carry well; they can be sliced easily, and the pastry covering tends to keep the filling together so that half of your picnic is not lost in the grass (or worse yet, the sand) if they are prepared correctly.

Ensure that pies and pastries are properly packed, for nothing is worse than a flattened pie, its crust broken and its filling seeping out onto other foods.

Pies come in all shapes and sizes. Large pies to be sliced can be baked in terrine or bread tins in the shape of that ubiquitous pub cliché, the veal and egg pie, or baked in circular loose-bottomed tins with spring clips which make unmoulding an easy affair. Individual pastries can either be baked in tartlet tins or without a tin at all, as in the classic Cornish pasty or the rather less familiar Turkish *borek*.

Various pastry doughs can also be used. Most usual would be a shortcrust pastry made from half wholemeal and half strong white bread flour, but some pies can be made using puff pastry or even filo pastry.

If you are not too particular about the slight flavour of margarine in commercial puff pastry, the bought wholemeal type seems to me a good idea, although the crust will always taste much the same and it does not take long to make your own, which will, without doubt, be superior in flavour and of which you can vary the taste at your own whim by adding herbs or spices. Making filo pastry from scratch, however, is one of the great skills of the pastry chef, so unless you are skilled in its preparation, it is better to buy it ready-made. Nearly every recipe using filo pastry tells you to smear each leaf generously with melted butter before adding the next, but this will give a quality to the finished pastry that is far too rich to certain palates and a product that is very high in saturated fat. You can obtain that buttery flavour by smearing every third or fourth sheet with butter, but I find that a very pleasant result is achieved with the use of a polyunsaturated oil such as sunflower, safflower or corn. Using oil instead of butter on every second sheet will give a moist but crisp finish that is not too rich. This is my preference, but it is all a matter of taste; you pays your money and you takes your choice.

As all these pastries will be served cold, you must consider how well the filling will slice. The pie must not be too dry or crumbly, nor should it be so moist that the filling will ooze out in a small pool. A sauce thickened with too much flour will be unpleasantly doughy when eaten cold and tends to spring back like a sponge as well. If fish is used in the filling, the sauce will probably jell, which is the best solution; if not, it can be helped with the addition of a jelly made from a reduced fish stock, agar-agar or gelatine.

Decorate your pies with pastry leaves or anything else which strikes your fancy. Pies are one of the most attractive foods that one can bring along for a picnic.

The Pastry

Pastrymaking entails simple, basic techniques which, once learned, can almost be done in one's sleep.

The dough should be wrapped in cling film or greaseproof paper, and it needs to be left to rest for a short period in a cool place or in the refrigerator for 30 minutes. This ensures that the gluten in the flour has time to relax and become pliable so that the dough will be more supple when it is rolled out. A small amount of ascorbic acid added to the pastry (a tablespoonful of lemon juice) also helps the gluten relax, and the end result will be lighter pastry. It also helps immeasurably for the ingredients to be cool or cold. I prefer to take the fat rock hard from the refrigerator and grate it into the flour, rather than cutting it up into small dice. This will shorten the preparation time, and even if you are using a food processor, this technique works very well.

It is well worth making pastry in large batches, as it freezes very well.

Too much water added to the dough will result in a hard, brittle paste, so use only as much as it necessary to bind the dough together.

Do not sprinkle a lot of flour on the pastry board when rolling out the dough, since this will distort the proportions of the ingredients.

Do not stretch the pastry to fit the pie dish or tin, because it will shrink back to its original size.

WHOLEMEAL SHORTCRUST PASTRY

Makes ¾ lb (340g). Enough to line one 10-inch round tin.

Preparation time: 15 minutes
Standing time: 30 minutes

IMPERIAL (METRIC)
½ lb (225g) wholemeal flour
Pinch of salt
2 oz (55g) unsalted butter
2 oz (55g) polyunsaturated margarine
1 tablespoonful lemon juice
2 scant tablespoonsful iced water

AMERICAN
2 cups wholemeal pastry flour
Pinch of salt
4 tablespoonsful unsalted butter
*4 tablespoonsful polyunsaturated
  margarine*
1 tablespoonful lemon juice
2 scant tablespoonsful iced water

1. Sift the flour into a large bowl, then shake the bran back into the flour. Add the salt, then grate the fats into the flour. Rub the fat and flour together with the tips of your fingers until the flour has absorbed all the fat and the mixture resembles crystals of sand. Add the lemon juice and mix to a paste, adding the water slowly until the dough holds together. (It is difficult to give a precise measurement of water, because wholemeal flour seems to absorb more liquid on some occasions than others, but this ratio of flour to fat (2:1) should give a rich, crumbly texture to the pastry if you have not added too much water.)
2. Form the dough into a ball, wrap with cling film or greaseproof paper and leave in a cool place or in the refrigerator for 30 minutes.
3. Roll out the pastry to a thickness of about ⅛ inch (3mm). Ease into the pie dish or tin, being careful not to stretch the pastry.

Variation: This pastry can be made using half wholemeal and half unbleached white flour. It can also be made entirely of white flour, which will give a very bland taste, but more crumbly texture. You can flavour the pastry with hard grated cheese or herbs in addition to the fats, or substitute part of the flour with oatmeal or buckwheat.

WHITE FISH PIE
Serves 4–6

Preparation time:	Making the pastry, plus 15 minutes
Cooking time:	45 minutes
Baking time:	45 minutes

IMPERIAL (METRIC)	AMERICAN
1 recipe quantity Wholemeal Shortcrust Pastry (page 101)	*1 recipe quantity Wholemeal Shortcrust Pastry (page 101)*
1 lb (455g) mixed heads and bones of white fish high in gelatine (see page 82)	*1 lb mixed heads and bones of white fish high in gelatine (see page 82)*
1½ lb (680g) white fish fillets (sole, plaice, monkfish, brill, rock salmon, turbot or halibut)	*1½ lb white fish fillets (sole, flounder, monkfish, brill, whitefish, turbot or halibut)*
2 oz (55g) butter	*4 tablespoonsful butter*
¼ pint (140) dry sherry	*⅔ cup dry sherry*
3 tablespoonsful finely chopped parsley	*3 tablespoonsful finely chopped parsley*
2 tablespoonsful capers	*2 tablespoonsful capers*
Sea salt and freshly ground black pepper	*Sea salt and freshly ground black pepper*
1 egg, beaten to glaze	*1 egg, beaten to glaze*

1. Roll out two-thirds of the pastry thinly and use to line the base and sides of a 2-lb/1kg/9 × 5 × 3-inch (22.5 × 12.5 × 7.5cm) bread tin.
2. Place the fish heads and bones in a large saucepan and cover with water. Bring to the boil over moderate heat, then reduce the heat and simmer for 30 minutes. Remove from the heat and remove the fish scraps with a slotted spoon and discard. Return the stock saucepan to the heat and reduce the liquid to ½ pint/285ml/1¼ cups over high heat. Remove from the heat and set aside to cool.
3. Preheat the oven to 425°F/220°C (Gas Mark 7).
4. Chop the fish fillets into small pieces. Melt the butter in a medium-sized saucepan over moderate heat and sauté the fish for a mere 2 minutes. Remove from the heat and stir in the sherry, parsley, capers, seasoning and the reduced fish stock. Pack this mixture tightly into the pastry case.
5. Roll out the remaining pastry and fit over the top of the pie, sealing the edges well. Glaze with the beaten egg.
6. Bake for 40–45 minutes. Remove from the oven and allow to cool.

Variations:

Smoked Fish Pie
Substitute undyed smoked haddock fillets for the white fish fillets.

Shellfish Pie
Substitute prawns and scallops for the white fish fillets.

Mushroom and Prawn Pie
Substitute 1½ lb (680g) prawns for the white fish fillets and add ½ lb (225g) sliced fresh mushrooms.

VEGETABLE PIE

Serves 4–6

Preparation time:	Making the pastry and baking blind, plus 15 minutes
Cooking time:	30 minutes
Baking time:	45 minutes

IMPERIAL (METRIC)

1 recipe quantity Wholemeal
Shortcrust Pastry (page 101)

Filling:
1½ lb (680g) potatoes
1 lb (680g) mushrooms
2 oz (55g) butter
3 cloves garlic, crushed
1 lb (455g) onions, thinly sliced
Generous handful of parsley, finely
chopped
1 tablespoonful lemon juice
3 tablespoonsful shoyu sauce
Sea salt and freshly ground black
pepper
1 egg, beaten to glaze

AMERICAN

1 recipe quantity Wholemeal
Shortcrust Pastry (page 101)

Filling:
1½ lb potatoes
1 lb mushrooms
4 tablespoonsful butter
3 cloves garlic, crushed
1 lb onions, thinly sliced
Generous handful of parsley, finely
chopped
1 tablespoonful lemon juice
3 tablespoonsful shoyu sauce
Sea salt and freshly ground black
pepper
1 egg, beaten to glaze

1. Roll out two-thirds of the pastry thinly and use to line the base and sides of a 9–10 inch (22.5–25cm) spring clip pie tin. Bake blind.

2. Peel the potatoes and boil in very little water until tender, about 15–20 minutes. Remove from the heat and drain well.

3. Slice the mushrooms thinly. Melt the butter in a large saucepan and sauté the mushrooms with the garlic and onions for 5 minutes. Meanwhile, dice the potatoes. Add the parsley and potatoes to the saucepan, then the lemon juice and shoyu sauce. Season to taste and mix well. Remove from the heat and pack into the pastry case.

4. Roll out the remaining pastry and cover the pie, sealing the edges well. Glaze with the beaten egg.

5. Bake for 45 minutes. Remove from the oven and allow to cool before unmoulding.

Variation:

Spiced Vegetable Pie
Add 1 tablespoonful garam masala and 1 oz/30g/1-inch piece grated root ginger to the butter and cook for a couple of minutes before adding the mushrooms. Proceed as above.

ONION TART

Serves 4–6

Preparation time:	Making the pastry and baking blind
Cooking time:	5 minutes
Baking time:	30 minutes

IMPERIAL (METRIC)	AMERICAN
¾ recipe quantity Wholemeal Shortcrust Pastry (page 101)	*¾ recipe quantity Wholemeal Shortcrust Pastry (page 101)*
Filling:	Filling:
1 oz (30g) butter	*2 tablespoonsful butter*
2–3 onions, sliced	*2–3 onions, sliced*
¼ teaspoonful grated nutmeg	*¼ teaspoonful grated nutmeg*
1 tablespoonful crushed juniper berries	*1 tablespoonful crushed juniper berries*
Sea salt and freshly ground black pepper	*Sea salt and freshly ground black pepper*
½ pint (285ml) smetana	*1¼ cups low-fat sour cream*
¼ pint (140ml) single cream	*⅔ cup light cream*

1. Roll out the pastry thinly and use to line the base and sides of a 9–10 inch (22.5–25cm) spring clip pie tin. Bake blind.
2. Preheat the oven to 400°F/200°C (Gas Mark 6).
3. Melt the butter in a medium-sized saucepan over moderate heat and cook the onions until softened, about 5 minutes. Remove from the heat.
4. Add the nutmeg, juniper berries, seasoning, smetana and cream to the onions. Mix well, then pour into the pastry case.
5. Bake for 30 minutes. Remove from the oven and allow to cool before unmoulding.

SIMPLE LEEK QUICHE

Serves 4–6

Preparation time:	Making the pastry and baking blind, plus 5 minutes
Cooking time:	5–8 minutes
Baking time:	20–25 minutes

IMPERIAL (METRIC)
¾ recipe quantity Wholemeal
  Shortcrust Pastry (page 101)

Filling:
1½ lb (680g) leeks
1 oz (30g) butter
3 eggs, beaten
2 oz (55g) Cheddar cheese, grated
1 tablespoonful thick cream
Sea salt and freshly ground black
  pepper

AMERICAN
¾ recipe quantity Wholemeal
  Shortcrust Pastry (page 101)

Filling:
1½ lb leeks
2 tablespoonsful butter
3 eggs, beaten
½ cup grated Cheddar cheese
1 tablespoonful thick cream
Sea salt and freshly ground black
  pepper

1. Roll out the pastry thinly and use to line the base and sides of a 9–10 inch (22.5–25cm) spring clip pie tin. Bake blind.
2. Preheat the oven to 400°F/200°C (Gas Mark 6).
3. Trim and clean the leeks. Slice thinly.
4. Melt the butter in a medium-sized saucepan over low heat and cook the leeks, covered, for 5–8 minutes, or until soft. Remove from the heat and allow to cool slightly.
5. Stir the eggs, cheese and cream into the leeks and season to taste. Pour the mixture into the pastry case and bake for 20--25 minutes. Remove from the oven and allow to cool before unmoulding.

COURGETTE TIAN

A tian is a quiche without pastry, so by rights, this recipe should not be in this chapter; but served cold, it is very easy to eat and very simple to make and it is a pie of sorts, so I have included it.

Serves 4–6
Cooking time: 8 minutes
Baking time: 20 minutes

IMPERIAL (METRIC)	AMERICAN
1 oz (30g) butter	*2 tablespoonsful butter*
1½ lb (680g) courgettes, sliced	*1½ lb zucchini, sliced*
3 eggs, beaten	*3 eggs, beaten*
2 oz (55g) Cheddar cheese, grated	*½ cup grated Cheddar cheese*
2 oz (55g) Gruyère cheese, grated	*½ cup grated Gruyère cheese*
Sea salt and freshly ground black pepper	*Sea salt and freshly ground black pepper*

1.   Preheat the oven to 400°F/200°C (Gas Mark 6). Butter a tian (shallow earthenware dish) or ovenproof dish.
2.   Melt the butter in a medium-sized saucepan. Cook the courgettes until soft, about 8 minutes. Remove from the heat and set aside to cool.
3.   Mix the eggs, Cheddar and Gruyère cheese into the courgettes and season to taste. Pour into the prepared dish and bake for 20 minutes or until brown and slightly risen. Remove from the oven and allow to cool before unmoulding.

SPINACH AND ALMOND TART

Serves 4–6
Preparation time: Making the pastry and baking blind
Cooking time: 8–10 minutes
Baking time: 30 minutes

IMPERIAL (METRIC)	AMERICAN
¾ recipe quantity Wholemeal Shortcrust Pastry (page 101)	*¾ recipe quantity Wholemeal Shortcrust Pastry (page 101)*
Filling:	Filling:
1 oz (30g) butter	*2 tablespoonsful butter*
1½ lb (680g) spinach	*1½ lb spinach*
½ pint (285ml) smetana	*1¼ cups low-fat sour cream*
¼ pint (140ml) single cream	*⅔ cup light cream*
¼ teaspoonful grated nutmeg	*¼ teaspoonful grated nutmeg*
Sea salt and freshly ground black pepper	*Sea salt and freshly ground black pepper*
2 oz (55g) flaked almonds	*½ cup slivered almonds*

1. Roll out the pastry thinly and use to line the base and sides of a 9–10 inch (22.5–25cm) spring clip pie tin. Bake blind.
2. Preheat the oven to 400°F/200°C (Gas Mark 6).
3. Melt the butter in a medium-sized saucepan over low heat and cook the spinach for 8–10 minutes, until soft. Remove from the heat and chop the spinach with a wooden spoon. Allow to cool.
4. Tip the spinach into a bowl and add the smetana, cream and nutmeg and season to taste. Pour the mixture into the pastry case and sprinkle with the almonds.
5. Bake for 30 minutes. Remove from the oven and allow to cool before unmoulding.

SMOKED HADDOCK QUICHE

Serves 4–6
Preparation time: Making the pastry and baking blind, plus 10 minutes
Cooking time: 5 minutes
Baking time: 30 minutes

IMPERIAL (METRIC)
¾ recipe quantity Wholemeal
   Shortcrust Pastry (page 101)

Filling:
1 oz (30g) butter
2 lb (900g) Finnan haddock
3 eggs, beaten
¼ pint (140ml) single cream
Sea salt and freshly ground black
   pepper

AMERICAN
¾ recipe quantity Wholemeal
   Shortcrust Pastry (page 101)

Filling:
2 tablespoonsful butter
2 lb Finnan haddie
3 eggs, beaten
⅔ cup light cream
Sea salt and freshly ground black
   pepper

1. Roll out the pastry thinly and use to line the base and sides of a 9–10 inch (22.5–25cm) spring clip pie tin. Bake blind.
2. Preheat the oven to 400°F/200°C (Gas Mark 6).
3. Melt the butter in a frying pan that will accommodate the haddock. Add the haddock and cook, covered, over low heat for 5 minutes. Remove from the heat and allow to cool. Reserve the cooking liquid.
4. Remove the fish skin and bones and flake the flesh into a bowl. Strain the cooking liquor into the bowl and add the eggs and cream and season to taste.
5. Pour the haddock mixture into the pastry case and bake for 30 minutes. Remove from the oven and allow to cool before unmoulding.

PIPERADE TART

Serves 4–6
Preparation time: Making and baking the pastry case
Cooking time: 30 minutes

IMPERIAL (METRIC)
1 9–10-inch (22.5–25cm) Wholemeal
Pastry Case, fully baked (use ¾ of
the recipe on page 101)

Filling:
2 tablespoonsful olive oil
2 green peppers, deseeded and sliced
2 onions, sliced
1 lb (455g) tomatoes, skinned and
chopped
3 eggs, beaten
Sea salt and freshly ground black
pepper
Handful of finely chopped parsley

AMERICAN
1 9–10-inch Wholemeal Pastry Case,
fully baked (use ¾ of the recipe
on page 101)

Filling:
2 tablespoonsful olive oil
2 green peppers, seeded and sliced
2 onions, sliced
1 lb tomatoes, skinned and chopped
3 eggs, beaten
Sea salt and freshly ground black
pepper
Handful of finely chopped parsley

1.   Heat the oil in a medium-sized saucepan over low heat. Add the peppers and onions and cook for about 20 minutes, until almost mushy. Add the tomatoes and cook for a further 5 minutes. Pour in the eggs, season to taste and scramble the eggs in the vegetable mixture until it thickens. Remove from the heat and cool slightly.
2.   Pour the vegetable and egg mixture into the pastry case and sprinkle with the parsley.

ARTICHOKE TART

Serves 4–6
Preparation time: Making the pastry and baking blind, plus 15 minutes
Cooking time: 45 minutes
Baking time: 30 minutes

IMPERIAL (METRIC)
¾ recipe quantity *Wholemeal*
   Shortcrust Pastry (page 101)
6 *large globe artichokes*
½ *pint (285ml) smetana*
¼ *pint (140ml) single cream*
Sea salt and freshly ground black
   pepper

AMERICAN
¾ recipe quantity *Wholemeal*
   Shortcrust Pastry (page 101)
6 *large globe artichokes*
1¼ *cups low fat sour cream*
⅔ *cup light cream*
Sea salt and freshly ground black
   pepper

1. Roll out the pastry thinly and use to line the base and sides of a 9–10-inch (22.5–25cm) spring clip pie tin. Bake blind.
2. Place the artichokes in a large saucepan (trimming the bases so they will stand upright). Bring to the boil and cook over moderate heat until tender, about 45 minutes. Remove from the heat, drain and allow to cool.
3. Preheat the oven to 400°F/200°C (Gas Mark 6).
4. Pluck out the leaves and scrape the edible flesh into a bowl. Cut out and discard the chokes. Chop the artichoke bottoms coarsely and add to the bowl. Add the remaining ingredients and mix thoroughly.
5. Pour the artichoke mixture into the pastry case and bake for 30 minutes. Remove from the oven and allow to cool before unmoulding.

TOMATO AND APPLE OATMEAL TART

Preparation time:	20 minutes
Cooking time:	20 minutes
Chilling time:	1 hour
Baking time:	30 minutes

IMPERIAL (METRIC)	AMERICAN
Pastry:	Pastry:
4 oz (115g) plain flour	*1 cup all-purpose flour*
4 oz (115g) rolled oats	*1 cup rolled oats*
1 teaspoonful sea salt	*1 teaspoonful sea salt*
4 oz (115g) butter or margarine	*½ cup (1 stick) butter or margarine*
1 large egg, beaten	*1 large egg, beaten*
Filling:	Filling:
1 lb (455g) tomatoes	*1 lb tomatoes*
2 dried red chillis	*2 dried red chili peppers*
¼ pint (150ml) red wine	*⅔ cup red wine*
2 oz (55g) butter	*4 tablespoonsful butter*
1 large onion, diced	*1 large onion, diced*
3 cloves garlic, crushed	*3 cloves garlic, crushed*
2 oz (55g) Cheddar cheese, grated	*½ cup grated Cheddar cheese*
1 large egg	*1 large egg*
3 tablespoonsful single cream	*3 tablespoonsful light cream*
Sea salt and freshly ground black pepper	*Sea salt and freshly ground black pepper*
2 dessert apples, peeled, cored and sliced	*2 eating apples, pared, cored and sliced*
1 onion, sliced and separated into rings	*1 onion, sliced and separated into rings*
2 oz (55g) grated Parmesan cheese	*½ cup grated Parmesan cheese*

1. Make the pastry in the usual manner. Line an 8–9-inch (20–22.5cm) tart tin with a removable base. Allow to rest for an hour or so in the refrigerator.
2. Make the filling. Cook the tomatoes, chillies and red wine together in a covered saucepan for about 10 minutes. Remove from the heat and allow to cool. Remove chillies and discard.
3. Preheat the oven to 375°F/190°C (Gas Mark 5).
4. Sieve the tomato mixture, then reduce the sauce by about one-half over a high heat. Remove from the heat and add the Cheddar cheese, egg and cream to the reduced tomato sauce. Mix well. Season with salt and pepper and pour into the pastry case.
5. Place the apples in a circular pattern on top of the sauce and cover with onion rings. Press down lightly so they are half-submerged. Sprinkle with the Parmesan cheese.
6. Place on a warmed baking sheet and bake for 30 minutes.

PRAWN FILO PIE

Serves 6
Preparation time: 30 minutes
Baking time: 35–40 minutes

IMPERIAL (METRIC)
20 Mediterranean prawns or *2½ lb*
   smaller prawns, cooked in their
   shells
¾ lb (340g) Ricotta cheese
½ lb (225g) Feta cheese, crumbled
2 large onions, finely chopped
2 tablespoonsful celery seed
1 teaspoonful celery salt
1 tablespoonful toasted sesame seeds
Sea salt and freshly ground black
   pepper
Generous handful of chopped parsley
1 lb (455g) frozen filo pastry, thawed
Melted butter or *sunflower oil to*
   brush pastry
Poppy seeds

AMERICAN
20 jumbo shrimp or *2½ lb smaller*
   shrimp, cooked in their shells
¾ lb Ricotta cheese
½ lb Feta cheese, crumbled
2 large onions, finely chopped
2 tablespoonsful celery seed
1 teaspoonful celery salt
1 tablespoonful toasted sesame seeds
Sea salt and freshly ground black
   pepper
Generous handful of chopped parsley
1 lb frozen filo pastry, thawed
Melted butter or *sunflower oil to*
   brush pastry
Poppy seeds

1. Peel the prawns. If using Mediterranean prawns, slice lengthways; leave smaller prawns whole. Set aside.
2. Place the Ricotta and Feta cheeses in a bowl and add the onions, celery seed, celery salt, sesame seeds, salt, pepper and parsley. Mix thoroughly.
3. Preheat the oven to 400°F/200°C (Gas Mark 6).
4. Unfold the filo pastry and cut the leaves in half with scissors (they will now be 9 × 12 inches (22.5 × 30cm). Grease a baking sheet with butter and place 7 or 8 leaves on the sheet, buttering or oiling every other leaf. Smear one-quarter of the cheese mixture over the pastry. Place another 7–8 leaves on top, buttering or oiling as before. Smear another quarter of the filling on top. Arrange the prawns evenly over this layer of cheese. Place more cheese mixture over the prawns and cover with 2 leaves of pastry. Brush with butter or oil and continue to stack the pastry as before, using up the remaining cheese mixture before laying on the last 8 pastry leaves, continuing to butter or oil every second leaf. Brush the top of the pastry with butter or oil and sprinkle with poppy seeds.
5. Bake for 35–40 minutes, or until the pastry is golden-brown. Remove from the oven and allow to settle for a few minutes before serving.

CRAB ROULADE

Serves 4–6
Preparation time: 30 minutes
Cooking time: 5 minutes
Baking time: 30 minutes

IMPERIAL (METRIC)
1 oz (30g) butter
10 sorrel or spinach leaves
½ lb (225g) frozen puff pastry,
  thawed
4 oz (115g) mozzarella cheese
Sea salt and freshly ground black
  pepper
½ lb (225g) white and brown crab
  meat
Generous handful of finely chopped
  parsley
Melted butter to brush pastry
Poppy seeds

AMERICAN
2 tablespoonsful butter
10 sorrel or spinach leaves
½ lb frozen puff pastry, thawed
4 oz mozzarella cheese
Sea salt and freshly ground black
  pepper
½ lb white and brown crab meat
Generous handful of finely chopped
  parsley
Melted butter to brush pastry
Poppy seeds

1. Melt the butter in a small saucepan over low heat. Add the sorrel or spinach and sauté until soft, about 5 minutes. Remove from the heat and purée with a wooden spoon.
2. Roll the pastry out thinly into a rectangle. Trim the edges.
3. Cut the mozzarella cheese into tiny cubes and mix with the sorrel or spinach purée. Season to taste. Spread over the pastry up to ½ inch (1.25cm) from the edges.
4. Season the crab meat and spread on top of the spinach mixture. Sprinkle with parsley.
5. Preheat the oven to 400°F/200°C (Gas Mark 6). Oil a baking sheet.
6. Roll up very gently as you would a Swiss roll, patting the filling down as you turn the pastry over. Place the roulade on the prepared baking sheet, seam-side down, and brush with melted butter. Sprinkle with a little sea salt and the poppy seeds.
7. Bake for 30 minutes until the pastry is well risen and golden-brown.

FILO MUSHROOM CROUSTADES

Serves 4–6

Preparation time: 10 minutes
Cooking time: 10 minutes
Baking time: 20 minutes

IMPERIAL (METRIC)	AMERICAN
4–5 sheets frozen filo pastry, thawed	*4–5 sheets frozen filo pastry, thawed*
1 oz (30g) butter	*2 tablespoonsful butter*
1 teaspoonful cumin seeds	*1 teaspoonful cumin seeds*
½ lb (225g) mushrooms, sliced	*½ lb mushrooms, sliced*
3 fl oz (90ml) dry red wine	*3 fl oz dry red wine*
Sea salt and freshly ground black pepper	*Sea salt and freshly ground black pepper*
5 oz (140g) cottage cheese	*⅔ cup cottage cheese*
Generous handful of chopped parsley	*Generous handful of chopped parsley*
1 egg, beaten to glaze	*1 egg, beaten to glaze*

1. Preheat the oven to 400°F/200°C (Gas Mark 6).
2. With a saucer, cut out rounds from the pastry. Grease a Yorkshire Pudding tin with butter and place 3–4 of the pastry circles in each hollow so that they overlap and hang over the top.
3. Melt the butter in a medium-sized saucepan over moderate heat. Add the cumin seeds and mushrooms and sauté for a few minutes. Reduce the heat and add the wine and seasoning. Cook for a further 5 minutes. Remove from the heat and allow to cool.
4. Add the cottage cheese and parsley to the mushroom mixture and mix well. Place a couple of tablespoonsful of this mixture into the pastry in the tins, then fold the pastry over so that the filling is completely enclosed. Brush with beaten egg.
5. Bake for 20 minutes or until the croustades are crisp and golden-brown.

FILO PURSES

Serves 4–6
Preparation time: 10 minutes
Cooking time: 20 minutes
Baking time: 20 minutes

IMPERIAL (METRIC)
1½ lb (680g) potatoes
1 oz (30g) butter
2 onions, thinly sliced
5 oz (140g) cottage cheese
2 oz (55g) Cheddar cheese, grated
Sea salt and freshly ground black
*   pepper*
4–5 sheets frozen filo pastry, thawed
Sunflower oil to brush pastry

AMERICAN
1½ lb potatoes
2 tablespoonsful butter
2 onions, thinly sliced
⅔ cup cottage cheese
½ cup grated Cheddar cheese
Sea salt and freshly ground black
*   pepper*
4–5 sheets frozen filo pastry, thawed
Sunflower oil to brush pastry

1. Scrub the potatoes, but do not peel. Place them in a medium-sized saucepan with a little water, bring to the boil, reduce the heat and cook until tender, about 20 minutes. Drain and cool, then dice into a bowl.
2. Meanwhile, melt the butter in a frying pan and sauté the onions until soft, about 5 minutes. Add to the potato together with the cottage cheese, Cheddar cheese and seasoning.
3. Preheat the oven to 400°F/200°C (Gas Mark 6).
4. With a saucer, cut out rounds from the pastry. Grease a Yorkshire Pudding tin with butter and place 4–5 of the pastry circles in each hollow, brushing each one with a little sunflower oil. Place about 2 tablespoonsful of the potato mixture in the centre of each tin over the pastry, then bring up the pastry in the shape of a purse to enclose the filling.
5. Bake for 20 minutes, or until the pastry is crisp and golden-brown.

AVOCADO AND ONION FLAN

Serves 4–6

Preparation time: Making and baking the pastry case, plus 10 minutes

Chilling time: 2 hours

IMPERIAL (METRIC)

1 9–10-inch (22.5–25cm) Wholemeal Pastry Case, fully baked (use ¾ of the recipe on page 101)

Filling:

5 oz (140g) cottage cheese
Handful of finely chopped parsley
1 bunch spring onions, finely chopped
Sea salt and freshly ground black pepper
1 tablespoonful lemon juice
Zest of 1 lemon, finely grated
2 ripe avocados
¼ pint (140ml) smetana
1 tablespoonful capers

AMERICAN

1 9–10-inch (22.5–25cm) Wholemeal Pastry Case, fully baked (use ¾ of the recipe on page 101)

Filling:

⅔ cup cottage cheese
Handful of finely chopped parsley
1 bunch scallions, finely chopped
Sea salt and freshly ground black pepper
1 tablespoonful lemon juice
Zest of 1 lemon, finely grated
2 ripe avocados
⅔ cup low fat sour cream
1 tablespoonful capers

1. In a bowl mix the cheese with the parsley, spring onions, seasoning, lemon juice and rind. Spread the mixture over the base of the pastry case.
2. Peel and stone the avocados and slice into strips. Place over the cheese in a circular pattern.
3. In a small bowl mix the smetana with the capers and cover the avocado strips.
4. Chill in the refrigerator for 2 hours.

PISSALADIÈRE

Serves 4–6

Preparation time: Making the pastry and baking blind, plus 5 minutes
Cooking time: 20 minutes
Baking time: 15 minutes

IMPERIAL (METRIC)
¾ *recipe quantity Wholemeal*
  Shortcrust Pastry (page 101)

Filling:
2 *tablespoonsful olive oil*
2 *onions, thinly sliced*
½ *teaspoonful dried oregano*
1 *lb (455g) tomatoes, skinned and*
  chopped
Sea salt and freshly ground black
  pepper
1 *tin anchovy fillets*
6 *black olives, stoned*

AMERICAN
¾ *recipe quantity Wholemeal*
  Shortcrust Pastry (page 101)

Filling:
2 *tablespoonsful olive oil*
2 *onions, thinly sliced*
½ *teaspoonful dried oregano*
1 *lb tomatoes, skinned and*
  chopped
Sea salt and freshly ground black
  pepper
1 *can anchovy fillets*
6 *pitted black olives*

1. Roll out the pastry thinly and use to line the base and sides of a 9–10-inch (22.5–25cm) spring clip pie tin. Bake blind.
2. Preheat the oven to 400°F/200°C (Gas Mark 6).
3. Heat the olive oil in a medium-sized saucepan over moderate heat. Add the onions and oregano and sauté for a few minutes until soft. Add the tomatoes and simmer for 15 minutes. Remove from the heat and season to taste.
4. Pour the tomato mixture into the pastry case and arrange the anchovy fillets in a lattice pattern on top. Cut the olives in half and place inside the squares formed by the lattice. Bake for 15 minutes.

8

SALADS

Now there are a far greater variety of salad leaves to choose from than ten or five years ago. I advise eating at least one salad of raw vegetables, leaves and fruits once a day, if not twice. Fresh raw foods keep their vitamins and minerals intact and give so much more nutritional benefit. Salads are also a refreshing addition to any picnic.

For a simple salad of tossed leaves, wash the leaves at home, dry thoroughly and carry in plastic bags. Make the dressing and keep in a screw-topped jar. The salad can be tossed in its plastic bag, but make sure it is well drained of moisture. Add a little of the dressing, re-tie the bag and shake until the leaves are glossy.

More complicated salads (or salads that are already dressed) can be carried in large screw-topped jars if a plastic bag is not strong enough.

Salads, of course, need not consist only of leaves – it all depends on what other dishes the picnic is comprised of. Salads can be substantial picnic fare, for example, potato or Russian Salad or other salads made with mayonnaise. Carry these salads in a plastic box with a tightly fitting lid and give them a good stir before serving, since they can become undesirably messy after a few hours of travelling.

Fruit and vegetable salads are particularly refreshing. Grain salads, such as Tabbouleh, should be dressed at home as they need time to marinate in the dressing, as do grated vegetable salads. Be circumspect when adding the dressing. Add just enough in flavour and moisten the salad; more can be added at the picnic. A salad swimming in oil, vinegar and water is an unhappy and unappetizing sight.

AVOCADO AND APPLE SALAD

Serves 4–6
Soaking time: overnight
Preparation time: 15 minutes

IMPERIAL (METRIC)	AMERICAN
2 ripe avocados	*2 ripe avocados*
2 dessert apples	*2 eating apples*
1 tablespoonful raisins, soaked overnight	*1 tablespoonful raisins, soaked overnight*
2–3 stalks celery, chopped	*2–3 stalks celery, chopped*
Zest and juice of 1 lemon	*Zest and juice of 1 lemon*
1 tablespoonful olive oil	*1 tablespoonful olive oil*
Sea salt and freshly ground black pepper	*Sea salt and freshly ground black pepper*

1. Peel, stone and slice the avocados into a bowl.
2. Core the apples and slice into the bowl. Pour over the lemon juice. Add the lemon zest olive oil and seasoning and toss carefully to prevent breaking up the avocados.
3. If desired, add a little garlic vinaigrette at the picnic site.

MIXED BEAN SALAD

Serves 4–6
Preparation time: minimal

IMPERIAL (METRIC)	AMERICAN
1 lb (455g) French beans, cooked and chopped	*1 lb green beans, cooked and chopped*
4 oz (115g) flageolet beans, cooked	*½ cup navy beans, cooked*
½ lb (225g) beansprouts	*½ lb bean sprouts*
Zest and juice of 1 lemon	*Zest and juice of 1 lemon*
1 teaspoonful celery salt	*1 teaspoonful celery salt*
Vinaigrette dressing to serve (optional)	*Vinaigrette dressing to serve (optional)*

1. In a bowl, toss all the salad ingredients together.
2. Add the vinaigrette dressing, if using, just before serving.

HARICOT BEAN SALAD

Serves 4–6
Preparation time: minimal after soaking
Marinating time: several hours

IMPERIAL (METRIC)
*½ lb (225g) dried red kidney beans,
    cooked*
*½ lb (225g) dried black beans,
    cooked*
*1 bunch spring onions, finely
    chopped (optional)*

AMERICAN
*1¼ cups dried red kidney beans,
    cooked*
1¼ cups dried black beans, cooked
*1 bunch scallions, finely chopped
    (optional)*

Dressing:
3 cloves garlic, crushed
1 tablespoonful red wine vinegar
3 tablespoonsful olive oil
1 teaspoonful celery salt
½ teaspoonful mustard powder
Freshly ground black pepper

Dressing:
3 cloves garlic, crushed
1 tablespoonful red wine vinegar
3 tablespoonsful olive oil
1 teaspoonful celery salt
½ teaspoonful mustard powder
Freshly ground black pepper

1. In a bowl mix together the kidney beans and black beans.
2. In a cup mix together thoroughly the garlic, vinegar, oil, celery salt, mustard powder and pepper.
3. Pour the dressing over the beans, toss and leave to marinate for several hours.
4. Just before serving, add the spring onions if using.

BROAD BEAN AND PEA SALAD

Serves 4–6
Preparation time: minimal after cooking beans

IMPERIAL (METRIC)
1 lb (455g) broad beans, cooked
1 lb (455g) garden peas, cooked
2 cloves garlic, crushed
3 tablespoonsful smetana
*2 tablespoonsful finely chopped
    parsley*
*Sea salt and freshly ground black
    pepper*

AMERICAN
1 lb fava beans, cooked
1 lb garden peas, cooked
2 cloves garlic, crushed
3 tablespoonsful low fat sour cream
*2 tablespoonsful finely chopped
    parsley*
*Sea salt and freshly ground black
    pepper*

1. In a bowl mix all the ingredients together.
2. Just before serving, stir well.

COLESLAW

Serves 4–6
Preparation time: minimal

IMPERIAL (METRIC)	AMERICAN
1 small white cabbage, grated	*1 small white cabbage, grated*
2 dessert apples, peeled and grated	*2 eating apples, pared and grated*
2 onions, thinly sliced	*2 onions, thinly sliced*
Zest and juice of 2 limes	*Zest and juice of 2 limes*
Sea salt and freshly ground black pepper	*Sea salt and freshly ground black pepper*
Vinaigrette dressing or *soured cream dressing to serve*	*Vinaigrette dressing* or *sour cream dressing to serve*

1. In a bowl mix all the salad ingredients together.
2. Just before serving, add the chosen dressing and toss well.

CARROT AND ROSE SALAD

Serves 4–6
Preparation time: minimal

IMPERIAL (METRIC)	AMERICAN
1 lb (455g) carrots, finely grated	*1 lb carrots, finely grated*
2 tablespoonsful rose water	*2 tablespoonsful rose water*
Sea salt and freshly ground black pepper	*Sea salt and freshly ground black pepper*
Vinaigrette dressing to serve	*Vinaigrette dressing to serve*
Rose petals to garnish	*Rose petals to garnish*

1. In a bowl, mix the carrots and rose water together. Season to taste.
2. Just before serving, toss with a little vinaigrette dressing and garnish with rose petals, which are edible.

Opposite: Haricot Bean Salad (page 119).
Overleaf: A Mediterranean Beach Picnic (pages 27 to 31).

CELERIAC AND CAULIFLOWER SALAD

Serves 4–6
Preparation time: minimal

IMPERIAL (METRIC)	AMERICAN
2 small celeriac roots, peeled and grated	2 small celeriac (celery root), pared and grated
1 small cauliflower, finely chopped	1 small cauliflower, finely chopped
Zest and juice of 1 lemon	Zest and juice of 1 lemon
1 bunch spring onions, thinly sliced	1 bunch scallions, thinly sliced
2 tablespoonsful smetana	2 tablespoonsful low fat sour cream
Sea salt and freshly ground black pepper	Sea salt and freshly ground black pepper

1. In a bowl mix the celeriac and cauliflower together. Add the lemon zest and juice and toss with the vegetables.
2. Just before serving, add the spring onions and smetana and season to taste.

CELERY, PEPPER AND ONION SALAD

Serves 4–6
Preparation time: minimal

IMPERIAL (METRIC)	AMERICAN
4–5 stalks celery, finely chopped	4–5 stalks celery, finely chopped
1 red pepper, deseeded and sliced	1 red pepper, seeded and sliced
1 green pepper, deseeded and sliced	1 green pepper, seeded and sliced
2 onions, thinly sliced	2 onions, thinly sliced
6 black olives, stoned and quartered	6 pitted black olives, quartered
Zest and juice of 1 lemon	Zest and juice of 1 lemon
Garlic vinaigrette dressing to serve	Garlic vinaigrette dressing to serve

1. In a bowl mix all the salad ingredients together.
2. Just before serving, toss with a little garlic vinaigrette dressing.

CHICORY AND ORANGE SALAD

Serves 4–6
Preparation time: minimal

IMPERIAL (METRIC)	AMERICAN
2–3 heads chicory	2–3 heads Belgian endive
2 oranges	2 oranges
2 oz (55g) broken walnuts	1/2 cup broken walnuts
Vinaigrette dressing made with walnut oil to serve	Vinaigrette dressing made with walnut oil to serve

1. Make this salad at the picnic site: separate the chicory leaves and peel and segment the oranges. Mix together with the walnuts.
2. Toss together well with a thick, oily vinaigrette made with walnut oil.

Opposite: Glazed Apple Tart (page 134).

CUCUMBER AND CELERY SALAD

Serves 4-6
Preparation time: minimal

IMPERIAL (METRIC)
1 cucumber, unpeeled, cubed
4-5 stalks celery, chopped
½ lb (225g) grapes, deseeded and
 halved
1 teaspoonful caraway seeds
Zest and juice of 1 lemon
Garlic vinaigrette dressing to serve

AMERICAN
2 cucumbers, unpared, cubed
4-5 stalks celery, chopped
½ lb grapes, seeded and halved
1 teaspoonful caraway seeds
Zest and juice of 1 lemon
Garlic vinaigrette dressing to serve

1. In a bowl mix the cucumber, celery, grapes and caraway seeds together.
2. Just before serving, toss gently with the garlic vinaigrette dressing.

FENNEL, TOMATO AND APPLE SALAD

Serves 4-6
Preparation time: minimal

IMPERIAL (METRIC)
2 fennel roots, cut into cubes
3 tomatoes, chopped
2 red dessert apples, cored and
 chopped
Zest and juice of 1 lemon
Vinaigrette dressing to serve

AMERICAN
2 fennel roots, cut into cubes
3 tomatoes, chopped
2 red eating apples, cored and
 chopped
Zest and juice of 1 lemon
Vinaigrette dressing to serve

1. In a bowl mix together the fennel, tomatoes, apples, lemon zest and juice.
2. Just before serving, toss with vinaigrette dressing.

MUSHROOM, CELERY AND EGG SALAD

Serves 4–6
Preparation time: minimal

IMPERIAL (METRIC)
½ lb (225g) mushrooms, thinly sliced
4–5 stalks celery, chopped
Zest and juice of 1 lemon
2 eggs, hard-boiled and chopped
Vinaigrette dressing to serve

AMERICAN
½ lb mushrooms, thinly sliced
4–5 stalks celery, chopped
Zest and juice of 1 lemon
2 eggs, hard-cooked and chopped
Vinaigrette dressing to serve

1. In a bowl mix together the mushrooms, celery, lemon zest and juice.
2. Just before serving, add the eggs and toss gently with the vinaigrette dressing.

RED CABBAGE AND APPLE SALAD

Serves 4–6
Preparation time: minimal

IMPERIAL (METRIC)
1 small red cabbage, grated
2 Granny Smith apples, unpeeled,
   grated
2–3 stalks celery, chopped
Zest and juice of 1 lemon
Vinaigrette dressing

AMERICAN
1 small red cabbage, grated
2 Granny Smith apples, unpeeled,
   grated
2–3 stalks celery, chopped
Zest and juice of 1 lemon
Vinaigrette dressing

1. In a bowl, mix together all the salad ingredients.
2. Just before serving, toss with the vinaigrette dressing.

SPRING SPINACH AND AVOCADO SALAD

Serves 4
Preparation time: 10 minutes

IMPERIAL (METRIC)
4 oz (115g) very young leaf spinach
1 handful rocket leaves
1 handful dandelion leaves
2 ripe avocados
Zest and juice of 1 lemon
Garlic vinaigrette to serve

AMERICAN
¼ lb very young leaf spinach
1 handful arugula (rocket-salad)
1 handful dandelion leaves
2 ripe avocados
Zest and juice of 1 lemon
Garlic vinaigrette to serve

1. Remove the spinach leaves from the stalks and discard the stalks. Tear the spinach leaves into small pieces.
2. Peel, stone and slice the avocados and toss with the lemon zest and juice.
3. In a bowl, gently mix the spinach, rocket and dandelion leaves with the avocados.
4. Just before serving, toss lightly with the garlic vinaigrette.

9

COOKING OUT OF DOORS

Fish
A whole barbecued fish is one of the most succulent dishes I can imagine. If it has just been caught, the flavour is so fresh and intense that it is a unique experience.

Fish can be barbecued over fennel or vine or rosemary twigs, which will flavour it.

Large fish can be slashed diagonally at intervals, the cuts rubbed with herbs, garlic or seasoning and the skin oiled to keep it from sticking to the grill. Small fish can be speared through the head with a skewer. One can buy a wire frame that will hold one large fish or several small fish that facilitates turning the fish so that it can cook evenly on both sides.

Never, but never, overcook fish. All fish need the briefest time in the heat so that the flesh just changes from raw to white. Any more cooking and the juices start to evaporate and the flavour and sweetness declines.

If you take a small box for home smoking to the picnic with you, fish can be smoked on the spot. The method is as follows: salt the fish briefly, then place in the box. Fill a tin with methylated spirit and place beneath the box, which is then shut tightly for 10-12 minutes. Fish can either be smoked whole or filleted.

You can also cook fish in the embers of a fire. Place the fish on a piece of aluminium foil large enough to enclose it completely. Add chopped fresh herbs and dot with butter, then seal the foil. The fish will be cooked through in 10-15 minutes. You can also stuff the fish with nuts, raisins and spices as in Middle Eastern methods of cooking.

Another outdoor method of grilling fish is to wrap it in leaves. First scale and gut the fish, stuff the cavity with butter, season and wrap in vine, spinach or cabbage leaves. Oil the leaves before placing on the grill.

Vegetables

Potatoes
Wrap in foil and cook in the embers of a fire: they will be done within an hour; or cook on top of the grill (they will have to be turned and will take longer to cook).

Sweet potatoes can be cooked using the same methods, but will require only half the cooking time.

Corn on the Cob
Corn can be roasted whole on a grill over a fire. It will take about 20 minutes, but turn the cobs so they are evenly done.

Peppers
Grill peppers whole so that the skin blisters and blackens. Scrape off the skin, then slice

and eat with vinaigrette dressing or butter. Peppers can also be sliced, skewered and grilled with other vegetables.

Aubergines
Use the same method as for cooking peppers. Aubergines will take longer to cook depending on the size. Again the skin will blister and blacken and the interior will be soft. You can either scrape out the flesh, mash it and mix with oil, lemon, garlic, and seasoning, or slice the aubergines before cooking, oil the slices and cook on the grill or on a skewer.

Onions
There are several methods for grilling onions. They can be cooked whole and the blackened outside skin discarded, or wrapped in foil and cooked in the embers like potatoes, or sliced and skewered with other vegetables in a kebab.

Courgettes
Courgettes may be cooked whole on top of the grill, or wrapped in foil and cooked in the embers (this should take 10 minutes) or used as an ingredient in a kebab.

Tomatoes
Tomatoes can be cooked whole on top of the grill if their skins are first pierced to prevent them from bursting; they can also be cut in wedges and skewered with other vegetables.

Mushrooms
Mushrooms can be cooked whole on top of the grill, skewered with other vegetables, or the caps filled with a simple stuffing consisting of butter, fresh herbs, garlic and breadcrumbs and cooked on top of the grill.

Tofu
Tofu can be cut into cubes and used with other vegetables in a kebab, or marinated in oil and herbs or curry sauce before being grilled. It can also be sliced and grilled on its own. There is a smoked tofu on the market now that is particularly suited to barbecue grilling.

SAUCES

I believe in simple, basic sauces that are no trouble to prepare, but still delicious. For picnics, it is best to consider a cold sauce, which can be carried in a screw-topped jar, rather than a hot sauce, which would require a separate vacuum flask. Barbecued fish and vegetables respond well to cold sauces, a few of which I offer here.

ONION AND GREEN PEPPERCORN SAUCE

Makes approximately ⅔ pint/340ml/1½ cups

| Marinating time: | 1 hour |
| Preparation time: | 5 minutes |

IMPERIAL (METRIC)
1 onion, finely chopped
2 tablespoonful green peppercorns
Sea salt and freshly ground black
  pepper
1 tablespoonful white wine vinegar
¼ pint (140ml) soured cream
¼ pint (140ml) natural yogurt

AMERICAN
1 onion, minced
2 tablespoonful green peppercorns
Sea salt and freshly ground black
  pepper
1 tablespoonful white wine vinegar
⅔ cup sour cream
⅔ cup plain yogurt

1. Place the onion, peppercorns, seasoning and vinegar in a bowl, mix and set aside for 1 hour. The onion will soften a bit, but not lose its bite.
2. Beat the soured cream and yogurt into the onion mixture.
3. This sauce will keep happily in a screw-topped jar.

SPICED PEANUT SAUCE

Makes ½ pint/285ml/1¼ cups

Preparation time: 10 minutes

IMPERIAL (METRIC)
1 teaspoonful Tabasco sauce
Zest and juice of 1 lemon
¼ pint (140ml) water
5 oz (140g) smooth peanut butter
Sea salt and freshly ground black
  pepper

AMERICAN
1 teaspoonful Tabasco sauce
Zest and juice of 1 lemon
⅔ cup water
½ cup smooth peanut butter
Sea salt and freshly ground black
  pepper

1. Pour the water into a small saucepan and add the lemon zest and juice and Tabasco sauce. Place over low heat. When the mixture is hot, slowly add the peanut butter, stirring until a smooth sauce is obtained.
2. Remove from the heat, season to taste and pour into a screw-topped jar. Allow to cool.

CURRY SAUCE

Makes approximately ⅔ pint/340ml/1½ cups
    Preparation time: 5 minutes, plus cooling

IMPERIAL (METRIC)
2 tablespoonsful sunflower oil
1 tablespoonful curry powder
1 teaspoonful powdered asafoetida
½ teaspoonful cumin seeds
½ teaspoonful caraway seeds
2 tablespoonsful lemon juice
¼ pint (140ml) soured cream
¼ pint (140ml) natural yogurt
Sea salt and freshly ground black
  pepper

AMERICAN
2 tablespoonsful sunflower oil
1 tablespoonful curry powder
1 teaspoonful powdered asafoetida
½ teaspoonful cumin seeds
½ teaspoonful caraway seeds
2 tablespoonsful lemon juice
⅔ cup sour cream
⅔ cup plain yogurt
Sea salt and freshly ground black
  pepper

1. Heat the sunflower oil in a frying pan over moderate heat. Add the spices and cook for 1–2 minutes. Remove from the heat and allow to cool.
2. Add the soured cream, lemon juice and yogurt to the spice mixture and season to taste. Mix thoroughly and pour into a screw-top jar.

AVOCADO SAUCE

Makes approximately ½ pint/285ml/1¼ cups
    Preparation time: 5 minutes

IMPERIAL (METRIC)
1 ripe avocado
¼ pint (140ml) soured cream
Zest and juice of 1 lemon
3 tablespoonsful finely chopped
  chives
Sea salt and freshly ground black
  pepper
Milk, if necessary

AMERICAN
1 ripe avocado
⅔ cup sour cream
Zest and juice of 1 lemon
3 tablespoonsful snipped chives
Sea salt and freshly ground black
  pepper
Milk, if necessary

1.   Peel and stone the avocado and scoop the flesh into a blender container. Add the soured cream and lemon zest and juice and blend to a purée. Add the chives and seasoning and blend again. If the sauce seems too thick, thin with a little milk.
2.   Pour into a screw-topped jar.

ANCHOVY SAUCE

Makes approximately ⅓ pint/200ml/1 scant cup

Preparation time: 5 minutes

IMPERIAL (METRIC)	AMERICAN
1 tin anchovies	*1 can anchovies*
Zest and juice of 1 lemon	*Zest and juice of 1 lemon*
1 tablespoonful shoyu sauce	*1 tablespoonful shoyu sauce*
¼ pint (140ml) water	*⅔ cup water*
Freshly ground black pepper	*Freshly ground black pepper*

1. Place the anchovies and their oil in a blender container. Add the remaining ingredients and blend to a smooth purée.
2. Pour into a screw-topped jar.

CAPER-LEMON SAUCE

Makes approximately ⅓ pint/200ml/1 scant cup

Preparation time: 5 minutes

IMPERIAL (METRIC)
3 tablespoonsful capers
Zest and juice of 2 lemons
¼ pint (140ml) water
Sea salt and freshly ground black
   pepper

AMERICAN
3 tablespoonsful capers
Zest and juice of 2 lemons
⅔ cup water
Sea salt and freshly ground black
   pepper

1. Place all the ingredients in a blender container and blend to a smooth purée.
2. Pour into a screw-topped jar.

10

INDOOR FOOD

A SUMMER DINNER PARTY

This meal begins with a light and very refreshing version of the Hungarian cherry soup. The main dish is an adaptation of the famous Greek moussaka, without meat; I cannot see much culinary value to any dish of a layer of minced meat, it is granular on the tongue and its flavour is thin. Better by far to make your moussaka out of just vegetables, and both leeks and okra are eaten widely in Greece. The broccoli dish, which stems from Italy, can be made with either cauliflower or calabrese, if you are a purist you can omit the anchovies, but then add a little salt. But if you do eat fish and this summer dinner party is wholly vegetarian, except for the anchovies, you might like to try the prawn dish described on page 111.

MENU FOR 4-6 PEOPLE

Cherry Soup
Leek and Okra Moussaka
Wild Rice with Summer Herbs
Sautéed Broccoli with Anchovies and Capers
Grilled Chèvre
Fruit Brulée

CHERRY SOUP

    Preparation time: 20 minutes
    Cooking time: 2 minutes and 2 hours refrigeration

IMPERIAL (METRIC)	AMERICAN
1 bottle of dry white wine	*1 bottle of dry white wine*
Grated rind of one lemon and the juice	*Grated rind of one lemon and the juice*
2 tablespoons of caster sugar	*2 tablespoons of caster sugar*
1 lb (450g) cherries	*1 lb cherries*

For the garnish:	For the garnish:
3 tablespoons fromage frais	*3 tablespoons fromage frais*
Handful of mint	*Handful of mint*
¼ pint (140ml) olive oil	*⅔ cup olive oil*
Juice of one lemon	*Juice of one lemon*
Teaspoon caster sugar	*Teaspoon caster sugar*
Sea salt and black pepper	*Sea salt and black pepper*

1. Empty a quarter pint (140ml) of the white wine into a pan and add the lemon rind, juice and caster sugar, heat until the sugar has melted and simmer for a few moments, leave to cool.
2. Over a blender jar, so as not to lose the juice, stone the cherries, place the cherry flesh into the jar and add the white wine.
3. Blend thoroughly, then add the melted sugar, wine and lemon, blend again.
4. Pour into a soup tureen and refrigerate.
5. To make the garnish, tear the leaves from the mint stalks and place in the blender with the olive oil, lemon, sugar, salt and pepper. Blend to a green sauce and finally stir in the fromage frais.

LEEK AND OKRA MOUSSAKA

    Preparation time: 1 hour
    Cooking time: 45 minutes

IMPERIAL (METRIC)	AMERICAN
2 large aubergines	*2 large aubergines*
1½ lb (675g) okra	*1½ lb okra*
1½ lb (675g) small leeks	*1½ lb small leeks*
1½ lb (675g) ripe tomatoes	*1½ lb ripe tomatoes*
4 oz (120g) parmesan, grated	*1 cup parmesan (grated)*
2 oz (50g) butter	*½ cup butter*
2 oz (50g) white flour	*½ cup white flour*
½ pint (280ml) milk	*1¾ cup milk*
3 tablespoons olive oil	*3 tablespoons olive oil*

1. Trim and slice the two aubergines into quarter-inch (½cm) pieces, then sprinkle them with salt and leave for an hour to exude their bitterness. Wash the salt off under a cold

tap, pat dry. Pour 3 tablespoons of olive oil into a pan and quickly fry the pieces so that they are just coloured.

2. Meanwhile, trim the leeks and wash any mud away from the green leaves. Slice them into 3-inch (8cm) lengths and throw them into a little heated boiling water and let them simmer for 2 minutes so that they are still *al dente*, drain and reserve. Wash the okra under a running tap and cook those like the leeks in a little boiling water for 2 minutes.

3. Slice the tomatoes in half and throw them into a pan with two cloves of chopped garlic and place over a low heat. Let them simmer so that they are reduced to a purée; this will take about 10 minutes. Put through a strainer or sieve to remove all the skins and pips which are thrown away.

4. Oil a shallow baking dish and lay half the aubergine slices on the bottom. Cover with the leeks and then the okra and pour over the tomato sauce. Sprinkle with half the parmesan and season with a little ground pepper and salt. Place the other half of the aubergine slices over the top.

5. Melt the butter, add the flour and make a roux, add the milk to make a sauce with the rest of the grated parmesan cheese. Pour over the top of the aubergines to cover, then place in a preheated oven 200°C/400°F/Gas Mark 6 for 40-45 minutes or until the inside is bubbling and it is golden brown on top. Take from the oven and let it rest for 5 minutes before serving.

WILD RICE WITH SUMMER HERBS

Preparation time: 10 minutes
Cooking time: 40 minutes

IMPERIAL (METRIC)	AMERICAN
8 oz (225g) wild rice	*8 oz wild rice*
Generous handful of parsley,	*Generous handful of parsley,*
chives or spring onions and	*chives or scallions and leaf*
leaf coriander, chopped fine	*coriander, chopped fine*

1. In a large saucepan bring to the boil 1½ pints (840ml, 3 cups) lightly salted water. Add the wild rice and simmer for about 40 minutes. The rice should not be too soft and still have plenty of bite to it.

2. Drain well and stir in the finely chopped herbs. Place a knob of butter in the middle before serving.

SAUTÉED BROCCOLI WITH ANCHOVIES AND CAPERS

Preparation time: 5 minutes
Cooking time: 8 minutes

IMPERIAL (METRIC)	AMERICAN
2 lb (900g) broccoli	*2 lb broccoli*
1 tin anchovies	*1 can anchovies*
3 tablespoons capers	*3 tablespoons capers*
3 tablespoons olive oil	*3 tablespoons olive oil*
3 tablespoons homemade toasted breadcrumbs	*3 tablespoons homemade toasted breadcrumbs*
1 tablespoon toasted pine nuts	*1 tablespoon toasted pine nuts*
Freshly ground black pepper	*Freshly ground black pepper*

1. Trim the stalks of the broccoli, leaving the florets intact, and throw into a pan of boiling salted water for 2-3 minutes. Drain carefully.
2. Heat the oil in a large frying pan and add the tin of anchovies so that they are broken up. Then throw in the broccoli and fry for another 2 minutes, adding the capers and the breadcrumbs in the last minute. Sprinkle before serving with a few toasted pine nuts.

GRILLED CHÈVRE WITH ROCKET

Preparation time: 5 minutes
Cooking time: 4 minutes

IMPERIAL (METRIC)	AMERICAN
6 slices chèvre about ⅛ inch (½cm) thick	*6 slices chèvre about ⅛ inch thick*
Generous handful of rocket leaves	*Generous handful of rocket leaves*

1. Choose a chèvre which is a cylinder so that the slices are round. Have the plates ready which will have the rocket leaves arranged on them.
2. Grill the chèvre slices on each side for about one minute so that they are just a little brown and runny. Serve immediately.

FRUIT BRULÉE

Preparation time: 10 minutes
Cooking time: 3 minutes

IMPERIAL (METRIC)	AMERICAN
1½ lb (675g) mixed summer fruit (strawberries, raspberries, red, black or white currants, grapes, plums, peaches)	*1½ lb mixed summer fruit (strawberries, raspberries, red, black or white currants, grapes, plums, peaches)*
8 fl oz (225g) thick double cream or fromage frais	*8 fl oz thick double cream or fromage frais*
4 oz (120g) soft brown sugar	*4 oz soft brown sugar*

1. Trim, stone and if necessary, chop the fruit and place mixture in the dish or dishes. Refrigerate at this stage.
2. Just before serving, light the grill, pour the cream or fromage frais over the surface of the fruit and sprinkle the top with a layer of brown sugar. When the grill is very hot, place the dish or dishes beneath it to caramelise the brown sugar. It should take just 30 seconds. Whip the dishes out immediately to the table.

LUNCH ON A RAINY DAY

Nothing is more maddening, when one has arranged a luncheon party in the garden and the weather becomes unreliable, suddenly there are clouds, chill winds and showers, when before there was sunlight. Summer food for entertaining then should be fairly flexible, one should have dishes which, though perfect for a cold buffet luncheon, can be adapted to be also warming and invigorating if you have to eat inside or under cover. This is a meal which should do both: the soup can be either hot or cold and many of the other dishes, as in Greece, can be eaten warm. The soup is made from rhubarb which continues to grow throughout the summer months. It is a highly acidic fruit which we generally associate only with puddings. To balance the acidity you will need a very strong vegetable stock, but you can now buy high class vegetable stock cubes (some are specifically low salt) which will do the job perfectly. This meal is also vegetarian, but I have added a fish dish which uses the same spices as the stir-fried vegetables and can be served with it, if people wish. Or the gingered monkfish can be served separately with wild rice on a different occasion.

MENU FOR 4-6 PEOPLE

Rhubarb Soup
Spiced Corn Muffins
Cucumber and Peanut Salad
Warm Potato and Garlic Salad
Stir Fry Summer Vegetables
English Summer Tabbouleh
Gingered Monkfish
A selection of cheeses and fresh fruits

RHUBARB SOUP

Preparation time: 5 minutes
Cooking time: 5 minutes

IMPERIAL (METRIC)
2 lb (900g) rhubarb, trimmed and sliced
2½ pints (1400ml) strong vegetable stock (use 4/5 salt-free cubes)
2 tablespoons light soy sauce
Freshly ground black pepper

AMERICAN
2 lb rhubarb, trimmed and sliced
6¼ cups stock (use 4/5 salt-free cubes)
2 tablespoons light soy sauce
Freshly ground black pepper

1. Heat the vegetable stock and throw in the rhubarb. Cook until it is soft, about 5 minutes. Leave to cool, then blend to a smooth purée.
2. Before serving, season with pepper and stir in the soy sauce. Serve if you like with a little sour cream or smetana and with the corn muffins below.

SPICED CORN MUFFINS

Makes 8-10 small muffins
Preparation time: 15 minutes
Cooking time: 20 minutes

IMPERIAL (METRIC)
3 oz (85g) sifted plain flour
2½ teaspoons baking powder
½ teaspoon salt
1 tablespoon sugar (optional)
5 oz (140g) corn meal
1 egg
4 oz (120g) Feta cheese, crumbled
2 green chillies, chopped small
3 tablespoons melted butter
6 fl oz (170ml) milk

AMERICAN
3 oz sifted plain flour
2½ teaspoons baking powder
½ teaspoon salt
1 tablespoon sugar (optional)
5 oz corn meal
1 egg
4 oz Feta cheese, crumbled
2 green chillies, chopped small
3 tablespoons melted butter
6 fl oz milk

1. Sift together flour, baking powder, salt and sugar. Then stir in corn meal and add the crumbled feta cheese and chopped chillies.
2. In a separate bowl, beat the egg thoroughly, then stir in melted butter and milk. Combine with the flour mixture, roughly stirring and not worrying if the batter is lumpy.
3. Spoon portions into a grased cake tin. Bake in a preheated 425°F/220°C/Gas Mark 7 oven for 20 to 25 minutes.

CUCUMBER AND PEANUT SALAD

Preparation time: 20 minutes

IMPERIAL (METRIC)	AMERICAN
3 large cucumbers	*3 large cucumbers*
5 tablespoons roasted peanuts	*5 tablespoons roasted peanuts*
A generous handful of chopped fresh coriander	*A generous handful of chopped fresh coriander*
A generous handful of chopped mint	*A generous handful of chopped mint*
2 teaspoons sugar	*2 teaspoons sugar*
Juice from one lemon	*Juice from one lemon*
½ teaspoon mustard seeds	*½ teaspoon mustard seeds*
½ teaspoon cumin seeds	*½ teaspoon cumin seeds*
½ teaspoon turmeric	*½ teaspoon turmeric*
½ teaspoon asafoetida	*½ teaspoon asafoetida*
2 green chillies	*2 green chillies*
2 tablespoons sunflower oil	*2 tablespoons sunflower oil*

1. Peel the cucumbers and scrape out the seeds. Grate the cucumber into a colander and squeeze out the excess moisture. Grind the roasted peanuts to a fine powder and add this with the coriander, mint, sugar and lemon juice to the cucumber.
2. Heat the sunflower oil in a pan and throw in the mustard and cumin seeds plus the sliced green chillies. Fry for a second or two, then add the turmeric and asafoetida, stirring quickly over the flame for a moment, then pour the contents over the salad. Add salt to taste and toss thoroughly, serve at once.

WARM POTATO AND GARLIC SALAD

Preparation time: 10 minutes
Cooking time: 45 minutes
(This is a delicious and troublefree recipe)

IMPERIAL (METRIC)	AMERICAN
2½ lb (1100g) salad potatoes (e.g. pink fir apple, rattes or charlotte)	*2½ lb salad potatoes (e.g. pink fir apple, rattes or charlotte)*
2 heads garlic	*2 heads garlic*
3 tablespoons olive oil	*3 tablespoons olive oil*
Sea salt and freshly ground black pepper	*Sea salt and freshly ground black pepper*

1. If the potatoes are small, about the size of walnuts, simply wash them under a running tap. If they are bigger, cut them into walnut size chunks but leave the peel on. Break up the two heads of garlic into separate cloves but do not peel the cloves.
2. Use a thick-bottomed iron casserole dish and heat the oil over a low flame, throw in the potatoes and the garlic cloves and put the lid on the pan. Keep the flame low and continue to cook for about 45 minutes, shaking the pan every now and then so that the potatoes do not stick. When they are cooked through, add the pepper and salt before serving and toss thoroughly.

STIR FRY SUMMER VEGETABLES

Preparation time: 15-20 minutes
Cooking time: 5 minutes

IMPERIAL (METRIC)	AMERICAN
10 garlic cloves, peeled and sliced	*10 garlic cloves, peeled and sliced*
2 oz (50g) ginger root, peeled and sliced finely	*2 oz ginger root, peeled and sliced finely*
2 red chillies, sliced thinly (omit stalk but use seeds and pith)	*2 red chillies, sliced thinly (omit stalk but use seeds and pith)*
1 tablespoon sunflower oil	*1 tablespoon sunflower oil*
1 tablespoon sesame oil	*1 tablespoon sesame oil*
1 lb (450g) tiny carrots	*1 lb tiny carrots*
1 lb (450g) baby leeks	*1 lb baby leeks*
1 lb (450g) courgettes	*1 lb zucchini*
1 bunch spring onions	*1 bunch scallions*
½ teaspoon sugar	*½ teaspoon sugar*
½ teaspoon salt	*½ teaspoon salt*
1 tablespoon dry sherry	*1 tablespoon dry sherry*
1 tablespoon light soy sauce	*1 tablespoon light soy sauce*

1. Prepare the carrots by trimming and slicing them into 4 lengthways. If the leeks are very small, trim them and use them whole. If larger, slice them in half lengthways. Slice the courgettes ⅛-inch (½cm) thick lengthways.
2. Heat the sunflower and sesame oil in a wok, then throw in the garlic, ginger and chillies. Fry for half a minute before adding the carrots and courgettes. Fry those for a minute then add the leeks, continue to fry shaking the wok and moving the vegetables around with a spatula for two more minutes. Then add the trimmed spring onions, sprinkle over with salt and sugar and toss the vegetables vigorously in the pan.
3. Finally add the sherry and soy sauce, turn off the heat and toss again thoroughly.
4. Turn out onto a platter. These are good at any temperature. Serve at once, allow to get warm or serve at room temperature. To complement this meal one needs a large mixed green salad, a variety of good native cheeses and fresh summer fruits to follow.

GINGERED MONKFISH

Preparation time: 15 minutes
Cooking time: 7 minutes

IMPERIAL (METRIC)	AMERICAN
2 lb (900g) monkfish tail, boned and cubed	*2 lb monkfish tail, boned and cubed*
Seasoned flour	*Seasoned flour*
1 tablespoon sesame oil	*1 tablespoon sesame oil*
2 tablespoons sunflower oil	*2 tablespoons sunflower oil*
2 oz (50g) ginger root, peeled and cut into julienne strips	*2 oz ginger root, peeled and cut into julienne strips*
2 green chillies	*2 green chillies*
3 cloves garlic, peeled and sliced	*3 cloves garlic, peeled and sliced*
2 tablespoons honey	*2 tablespoons honey*
1 tablespoon soya sauce	*1 tablespoon soy sauce*
1 tablespoon wine vinegar	*1 tablespoon wine vinegar*

1. Toss the pieces of monkfish in the seasoned flour, heat the sesame and sunflower oil and throw in the ginger, chillies and garlic, cook for a second or two before adding the fish.
2. Stir fry for several minutes, the fish should be cooked through in three minutes or thereabouts, then pour over the honey, soya sauce and wine vinegar, raise the heat and shake the pan vigorously so that all the pieces are covered.

ENGLISH SUMMER TABBOULEH

Preparation time: 15 minutes plus 1 hour's soaking

IMPERIAL (METRIC)	AMERICAN
8 oz (225g) bulgar wheat	*8 oz bulgar wheat*
4 fl oz (100ml) lemon juice	*4 fl oz lemon juice*
4 fl oz (100ml) olive oil	*4 fl oz olive oil*
3 cloves garlic, crushed	*3 cloves garlic, crushed*
1 bunch spring onions, chopped	*1 bunch scallions, chopped*
1 lb (450g) garden peas, boiled briefly	*1 lb garden peas, boiled briefly*
1 small punnet redcurrants, destalked	*1 small punnet redcurrants, destalked*
Bunch of fresh parsley, finely chopped	*Bunch of fresh parsley, finely chopped*
Bunch of fresh mint, finely chopped	*Bunch of fresh mint, finely chopped*
Bunch of fresh chives, finely chopped	*Bunch of fresh chives, finely chopped*
Sea salt and freshly ground black pepper	*Sea salt and freshly ground black pepper*

1. Soak the bulgar wheat in cold water for an hour, then drain and squeeze out all excess water. Take care over this, as you do not want a watery salad.
2. Mix the lemon juice, oil and garlic together in a large salad bowl, add the swollen bulgar wheat, toss thoroughly then add all the other ingredients.

11

DESSERTS

My favourite ending for picnic meals is cheese and fruit, since there is so much of both to choose from. Seasonal summer fruits make superb fruit salads which can be made on the spot, or just enjoy the fruit's natural sweetness *au naturel*. There is a very wide range of British cheeses that are delicious to eat and well worth taking on a picnic. For strict vegetarians concerned about animal rennet, there are more and more interesting cheeses now being made with plant rennet. Cornish *Yarg*, wrapped in nettle leaves, is one of the best. Then, of course, there is a huge variety of French cheese, plus local cheese from other countries. Many cheese connoisseurs claim that the most superior cheese is Cheddar, but it must be mature. Ending a meal with a good Cheddar, a little home-made pickle and a ripe pear or an apple seems like a good idea to me – there are few ways to improve on such a conclusion to a picnic.

Authors of picnic cookery books cannot resist offering recipes for puddings and desserts, but most puddings do not travel well, being too delicate and fragile. Fruit tarts are an exception. They can be made, glazed and packed carefully. Fruit or chocolate mousses are another possibility; they can be made in the container they will travel in, chilled until they are set, covered with a tightly fitting lid and packed with great care. If you are certain the lid on the container you are using can be relied on not to become loose, fruit fools and fruit salads can also be transported to a picnic, but they require a cool box or bag.

143

GLAZED APPLE TART

Makes 1 8-inch (20cm) tart
Preparation time: 20 minutes
Waiting time: 1½ hours
Baking time: 30 minutes

IMPERIAL (METRIC)
Rich Shortcrust Pastry:
6 oz (170g) plain flour
Pinch of sea salt
1 tablespoonful icing sugar
3 oz (85g) cold butter
2 egg yolks
A little iced water

Filling:
1 lb (455g) dessert apples
2 tablespoonsful castor sugar

Glaze:
3 tablespoonsful apricot jam or *fruit*
   jelly
2 tablespoonsful water
1 tablespoonful lemon juice

AMERICAN
Rich Shortcrust Pastry:
1½ cups all-purpose flour
Pinch of sea salt
1 tablespoonful confectioner's sugar
6 tablespoonsful cold butter
2 egg yolks
A little iced water

Filling:
1 lb eating apples
2 tablespoonsful superfine sugar

Glaze:
3 tablespoonsful apricot jam or *fruit*
   jelly
2 tablespoonsful water
1 tablespoonful lemon juice

1. First make the pastry. Sift the flour into a bowl and add the icing sugar and salt. Mix, then grate the butter into the flour mixture. Mix to the consistency of dry breadcrumbs.
2. Make a well in the centre of the flour mixture and stir in the egg yolks. Add enough iced water, little by little, to make a paste that will just hold together. Form into a ball, wrap in cling film and chill in the refrigerator for 1 hour.
3. Bring the dough back to room temperature. Roll out thinly and use to line the base and sides of an 8-inch (20cm) tart tin.
4. Preheat the oven to 350°F/180°C (Gas Mark 4).
5. Make the filling. Peel and core the apples and slice into the pastry case until it is full (you may need an additional apple). Sprinkle with castor sugar.
6. Bake the tart for 30 minutes. Meanwhile, prepare the glaze. In a small saucepan, melt the jam or jelly with the water and lemon juice over low heat.
7. When the tart is baked, remove from the oven and pour over the glaze. Leave to cool.

FOOLS AND SIMPLE MOUSSES

Soft fruits make beautiful fools. Cook 1 lb (455g) soft fruit briefly in its own steam; add no additional liquid. When the fruit is cooked, sweeten to taste with honey or sugar. It can then be puréed or not, depending on personal taste. Whip ½ pint/285ml/1¼ cups double cream and fold into the fruit. Cool the mixture and keep it in a container with a tightly fitting lid.

To make a simple fruit mousse, prepare the fruit as above, but instead of folding in whipped cream, whisk 2 egg whites until stiff and fold into the fruit, which can be set with either agar-agar or gelatine.

CHOCOLATE AND ORANGE MOUSSE

Serves 4-6
Preparation time: 10 minutes
Cooking time: 10 minutes
Chilling time: 2 hours

IMPERIAL (METRIC)
4 oz (115g) good quality plain chocolate
Zest and juice of 2 oranges
2 teaspoonsful gelatine or *agar-agar*
3 eggs, separated
2 oz (55g) castor sugar
¼ pint (140ml) double cream

AMERICAN
4 oz good quality bittersweet chocolate
Zest and juice of 2 oranges
2 teaspoonsful gelatine or *agar-agar*
3 eggs, separated
¼ cup superfine sugar
⅔ cup heavy cream

1. Melt the chocolate in an ovenproof dish in a cool oven or in the top of a double saucepan.
2. If using agar-agar, pour the orange juice into a small saucepan, stir in the agar-agar, bring to the boil over low heat and simmer for 4-5 minutes. If using gelatine, dissolve it in the orange juice over low heat.
3. In a bowl, mix together the egg yolks, orange zest and castor sugar. When it is thoroughly combined, stir in the orange juice mixture, then stir this mixture into the melted chocolate. Blend thoroughly, then fold in the cream. Pour into a container and chill in the refrigerator for about 2 hours to allow the mousse to set.

OTHER DESSERT IDEAS

Some of the nicest desserts can be made from low fat soft cheese, mixed with either a little cream, smetana or yogurt (depending on how keen you are about monitoring your fat intake).

Marinate some dried chopped fruit – raisins, currants or apricots, for example – in the spirit of your choice: sherry, Beaumes de Venise, walnut liqueur, cassis or whatever. Allow the fruit to marinate overnight, then beat in a mixture of low fat cheese, 2 tablespoonsful cream and 1 tablespoonful castor sugar or honey. Place into a mould and chill in the refrigerator until it is nicely set. Unmould this dessert at the picnic and decorate with chopped nuts.

12

HOME BAKING

Baking your own loaves is so much easier since the advent of micronized yeast (packaged under names like 'Easi-Bake'). This yeast should be added to the other dry ingredients and mixed, then warm water added. (The yeast will not become active until there is moisture.) This yeast does not need sugar to start it off, but its activity can be hindered by the addition of too much salt. Dough made with micronized yeast needs only one proving.

For a picnic, I find it pleasant to bake loaves I cannot buy in the shops, so I am including a few of these recipes.

Remember, if you use only wholemeal flour, the loaf will tend to be heavy and rise slowly. Half wholemeal flour and half plain flour makes a nicely texture loaf that will rise very quickly, although the flavour tends to be a bit dull, even when using unbleached, stoneground plain flour. I like to add herbs to this mixture – celery seeds, rosemary, dill or even garlic – to obtain a savoury loaf. It is excellent fresh and even better toasted and eaten with a vegetable or fish pâté. If you have an open fire at your picnic, toasting such a loaf is a memorable way of beginning the meal.

Another delicious loaf to bring to a picnic is the Cheese Brioche (page 149), which is somewhere between a bread, a sponge and a soufflé – rather rich, but excellent as a treat.

It is worthwhile to invest in a food mixer which includes dough hooks. This eliminates the chore of kneading the dough.

HERB BREAD
Makes 1 loaf

Preparation time:	15 minutes
Rising time:	45 minutes-1¾ hours, depending on type of yeast used
Baking time:	45 minutes

IMPERIAL (METRIC)	AMERICAN
½ lb (225g) strong unbleached white bread flour	2 cups unbleached white bread flour
½ lb (225g) wholemeal flour	2 cups wholewheat flour
½ teaspoonful dried rosemary	½ teaspoonful dried rosemary
½ teaspoonful dried sage	½ teaspoonful dried sage
½ teaspoonful dried marjoram	½ teaspoonful dried marjoram
½ teaspoonful celery salt	½ teaspoonful celery salt
1 sachet micronized yeast	1 package active dry yeast and 1 teaspoonful sugar dissolved in ¼ cup tepid water
2 tablespoonsful olive oil	2 tablespoonsful olive oil
Scant ½ pint (270ml) warm water	Scant cup warm water

1. Sift the white and wholemeal flours into a bowl, then shake back the bran. Add the micronized yeast, herbs and celery salt and mix thoroughly.
2. Add the oil and water (and dry yeast mixture, if using), mix and knead for 6-8 minutes, until the dough is elastic.
3. If using ordinary yeast, form the dough into a ball, place back into the bowl, cover and allow to rise in a warm place, free from draughts, for 1 hour, until double in bulk. If using micronized yeast, go on to the next step.
4. Grease a 1½-lb (680g) bread tin, fit the dough into the tin and leave to rise to the top of the tin, about 45 minutes.
5. Preheat the oven to 425°F/220°C (Gas Mark 7).
6. Bake the bread for 45 minutes. Test to see that it is done by tapping the bottom of the loaf. If it sounds hollow, remove from the oven and cool on a wire rack. If not, return to the oven for another 5-10 minutes.

CHEESE BRIOCHE

Makes 1

Preparation time: 10 minutes
Rising time: 1 hour
Baking time: 20-25 minutes

IMPERIAL (METRIC)	AMERICAN
10 oz (285g) strong *unbleached white bread flour*	2½ cups *unbleached white bread flour*
4 oz (115g) *butter, cut into small dice*	1 stick (4 oz) *butter, cut into small dice*
1 teaspoonful *sea salt*	1 teaspoonful *sea salt*
4 oz (115g) *mature Cheddar cheese, grated*	1 cup *grated aged Cheddar cheese*
3 eggs, *beaten*	3 eggs, *beaten*
2 tablespoonsful *milk*	1 package *active dry yeast and 1 teaspoonful sugar dissolved in 2 tablespoonsful tepid milk*
1 sachet *micronized yeast*	

1. In a bowl, mix together the flour, butter, salt and cheese, letting the flour absorb the butter and cheese.
2. Add the eggs, milk and micronized yeast (or yeast mixture) and knead for 5 minutes. As this dough is very sticky, it is easier to use a food mixer fitted with a dough hook.
3. Butter a brioche or bread tin, fit the dough into the tin and leave to rise in a warm place, free from draughts, for 1 hour.
4. Preheat the oven to 375°F/190°C (Gas Mark 5) for 20-25 minutes. Remove from the oven and cool on a wire rack.

WELSH FRUIT LOAF

Makes 1 loaf

Preparation time:	15 minutes
Rising time:	1-2 hours depending on type of yeast used
Baking time:	30 minutes

IMPERIAL (METRIC)	AMERICAN
3 oz (85g) butter	*6 tablespoonsful butter*
¼ pint (140ml) milk	*3 fl oz milk*
3 oz (85g) seedless raisins	*½ cup seedless raisins*
3 oz (85g) dried currants	*½ cup dried currants*
2 oz (55g) mixed candied peel	*Scant ½ cup mixed candied peel*
2 oz (55g) soft brown sugar	*½ cup soft brown sugar*
1 lb (455g) wheatmeal 81% extraction flour	*4 cups wholewheat 80% extraction flour*
1 teaspoonful sea salt	*1 teaspoonful sea salt*
1 teaspoonful ground mixed spice	*1 teaspoonful ground allspice*
1 sachet micronized yeast	*1 package active dry yeast and 1 teaspoonful sugar dissolved in ¼ cup warm milk*

1. Place the butter in a medium-sized saucepan and add the milk. Heat over low heat until the butter has melted. Add the raisins, currants, candied peel and sugar and warm through. Remove from the heat.
2. In a bowl, mix the flour, micronized yeast, salt and mixed spice, then add the milk and fruit mixture (and ordinary yeast if using). Mix together and knead for 5 minutes. (If using ordinary yeast, form the dough into a ball, return to the bowl, cover and leave to rise until doubled in bulk, about 1 hour. If using micronized yeast, go on to the next step.)
3. Butter a 2 lb (1kg) bread tin and place the dough in it. Leave to rise in a warm place, free from draughts, for 1 hour, or until the dough has risen to the top of the tin.
4. Preheat the oven to 400°F/200°C (Gas Mark 6).
5. Bake the loaf for 30 minutes, protecting the top with a piece of buttered greaseproof paper for the last 10 minutes. Remove from the oven and cook on a wire rack.

INDEX